PRINCIPLES AND PRACTICALITIES OF INTERFAITH RELATIONSHIPS IN NIGERIA

PRINCIPLES AND PRACTICALITIES OF INTERFAITH RELATIONSHIPS IN NIGERIA

(Interfaith Series, Vol. III)

Hyacinth Kalu

iUniverse, Inc.
Bloomington

PRINCIPLES AND PRACTICALITIES OF INTERFAITH RELATIONSHIPS IN NIGERIA
(Interfaith Series, Vol. III)

iUniverse books may be ordered through booksellers or by contacting:

iUniverse
1663 Liberty Drive
Bloomington, IN 47403
www.iuniverse.com
1-800-Authors (1-800-288-4677)

Because of the dynamic nature of the Internet, any web addresses or links contained in this book may have changed since publication and may no longer be valid. The views expressed in this work are solely those of the author and do not necessarily reflect the views of the publisher, and the publisher hereby disclaims any responsibility for them.

Any people depicted in stock imagery provided by Thinkstock are models, and such images are being used for illustrative purposes only.
Certain stock imagery © Thinkstock.

ISBN: 978-1-4620-2944-0 (pbk)
ISBN: 978-1-4620-2945-7 (ebk)

Library of Congress Control Number: 2011909596

Printed in the United States of America

iUniverse rev. date:06/10/2011

To my sisters:
Maureen Nina Kalu
And
Agnes Chikaodinaka Kalu

CONTENTS

LIST OF ABBREVIATIONS

ACRA	Advisory Council on Religious Affairs
ACYDF	African Christian Youths Development Forum
AIDS	Acquired Immune Deficiency Syndrome
ATR	African Traditional Religion
CAN	Christian Association of Nigeria
CBO	Catholic Boys' Organization
CCC	Catechism of the Catholic Church
CCN	Christian Council of Nigeria
HIV	Human Immunodeficiency Virus
LGA	Local Government Area
NAN	News Agency of Nigeria
NCC	National Communications Commission
NGO	Non-Governmental Organization
NIFAA	Nigerian Inter-Faith Action Association
NIPPS	National Institute for Policy and Strategic Studies
NIREC	Nigeria Inter-religious Council
NIYF	Nigerian Interfaith Youth Forum
NPO	Non Profit Organization
NSCIA	Nigeria Supreme Council for Islamic Affairs
NT New	Testament
NYSC	National Youth Service Corp.
OAIC	Organization of African Instituted Churches
OT	Old Testament
SCIA	Supreme Council of Islamic Affairs
SSS	State Security Service
St.	Saint
USA	United States of America
Vatican II	Second Vatican Council
VS	VERSUS

INTRODUCTION.

Over the years, interfaith relationships in Nigeria have been approached and treated from a dialogical point of view limited only to Christian-Muslim relationships or Christian-African Traditional Religious relationships. Unfortunately, this approach has not yielded the much needed tolerance, relationships, and collaborations among the three religions in Nigeria (African Traditional Religion (ATR), Islam and Christianity) because a major religion is always left out in these dialogues.

Given the amazing interest in interfaith relationships among the religions in Nigeria, and the desire to proffer a better approach to these relationships , this book proposes a trialogical approach as a partial solution to the religious conflicts and crises that have become the order of the day among the three religions in Nigeria. In this approach no religions is left out; all (ATR, Islam, and Christianity) are treated as equal partners in seeking and offering solution towards better relationships among religious followers and the Nigerian people. Interfaith relationships and activities involving all three religions in Nigeria (ATR, Islam and Christianity) without excluding any, is a powerful tool for promoting religious harmony, peace and cooperation for the stability and advancement of our nation. I came to this realization and conclusion through my personal experiences and involvements in trialogical interfaith and interactional relationships with these three religions: ATR, Christianity and Islam.

Furthermore, as the world is moving towards a global community, Nigeria is not left out. Hence, the problem of religion in Nigeria raises the question: how can the Igbo South East Christians live peacefully and enjoy all the benefits of the nation in the Muslim North, and how can the Northern Muslims live peacefully in the traditional Igbo East and Yoruba West, and enjoy the benefits of Nigerian citizens, while still maintaining publicly their religious identity? The answer and solution to this problem, I strongly believe, can only be found in interfaith relationships among the three religions in Nigeria.

Looking at the things that divide us and those that unite us, this book calls on followers of the different religions to move beyond their differences and work together in the spirit of interfaith relationships to make Nigeria better. It is pertinent at this point to emphasize that the focus of interfaith relationships among the religions in Nigeria is not aimed at proselytization, evangelization and apologetics. Rather, it is aimed at promoting mutual understanding and respect among the faith communities; an understanding and respect that will reduce religious bigotry, intolerance, violence and conflict, while promoting harmony, cooperation, friendship, tolerance and a peaceful society. This is exactly what Amir Hussain meant when he implied that interfaith relationships are not conversion, but an understanding and appreciation of the beauty and richness of the traditions of each other's faith, in which "we begin to understand our common heritage that can lead us to work together on a common future."[1]

Moreover, interfaith activities that embrace both the grass roots and the religious leadership of communities offer solutions to problems where political and diplomatic approaches have failed. This is because most of the religious problems in Nigeria occur at the grass-roots level and a better solution must include the same grassroots. Political and diplomatic approaches are mostly at the level of intellectuals and committees, and mostly exclude the grassroots.

The previous volume (Vol. II) in this series, on the one hand, discussed the horrible incidents of religious violence in Nigeria,

---

[1] Amir Hussain, *Oil and Water: Two Faiths, One God.* (Ontario, Canada: CopperHouse, 2006), 198.

occasioned partly as result of poor relationships among the three religions. It also, on the other hand, discussed the positive gains and improvements achieved, mostly through trialogical relationships, towards building a more harmonious religious and social environment for the Nigerian nation and people. This last volume, among other things, discusses in practical terms how, through interfaith activities, the three religions in Nigeria can have a better understanding of each other. It discusses the guidelines that will promote harmonious relationships and advance the cause of peace and development in Nigeria. Above all, it points out ways of working together and harmoniously to prevent future occurrences of religious conflicts and violence, which have so far dealt seriously blows to the nation and tainted the credibility of the three religions in Nigeria.

For convenient sake, this last volume is divided into six chapters. Chapters one through three provide the guidelines, commitments and suggested activities for fruitful trialogical interfaith relationships among the three religions in Nigeria. Chapter four points out and examines possible obstacles towards interfaith relationships and how best to deal with and avoid these obstacles.

Finally, chapters five and six re-assess what has been said and done so far. These chapters look into the future of Nigeria as a nation in connection with religion: its peace, stability, and well-being of its citizens, and what role religion has to play in it. They evaluate the past and propose ways forward.

CHAPTER ONE

GUIDELINES FOR INTERFAITH RELATIONSHIPS
AMONG THE THREE RELIGIONS IN NIGERIA.

Interfaith relationships do not take place in a vacuum; as the name indicates, it involves interpersonal and interreligious encounters and relations among followers of the three religions in Nigeria: African Traditional Religion, Islam and Christianity. As such there is need to lay careful ground rules as guiding principles that will regulate and direct the activities of participants so that better results may be achieved.

Looking at the religious scenario in Nigeria, the following are guidelines that should be adhered to for successful, fruitful and meaningful interfaith relationships among the three religions in Nigeria.

1. From dialogue to trialogue
2. Putting in place programs that encourage and promote interpersonal encounters
3. Acceptance, respect and recognition of the values of each other
4. Equality of all participants
5. Inclusive/parallel tendency rather than exclusive tendency

6. Seek issues and activities based more on common grounds and on what unites rather than what divides the three religions.
7. Being sensitive, honest, straightforward and open-hearted
8. Recognize and then forgive wrongs of the past
9. Reference the UN Declaration on the elimination of all forms of intolerance and discrimination based on religion and belief, and the Nigerian Constitution on religious freedom.

1.1 From dialogue to trialogue.

The key word that should guide interfaith relationships in Nigeria must of necessity be trialogue rather than dialogue. What do we mean by dialogue and trialogue, and how do they differ in the interfaith relationship? According to the popular usage of the word, dialogue connotes a two-way discussion involving ordinarily two people or groups. According to the *Merriam Webster Online Dictionary*, dialogue is a "conversation between two or more persons; an exchange of ideas and opinions; a discussion between representatives of parties to a conflict that is aimed at resolution."[2] In addition to the above definition, *Dictionary.com* adds the following clarifications,

> Dialogue is an exchange of ideas or opinions on a particular issue, especially a political or religious issue, with a view to reaching an amicable agreement or settlement. It means to discuss areas of disagreement frankly in order to resolve them.[3]

To analyze these two definitions within our religious context, dialogue in Nigeria has meant discussion between only two

---

[2]   "dialogue" *Merriam-Webster Online Dictionary*. 2008. http://www. merriam-webster.com/dictionary/dialogue (accessed: November 2, 2008)

[3]   Dialogue. Dictionary.com. *Dictionary.com Unabridged* (v 1.1). Radom House, Inc. http://dictionary.reference.com/browse/dialog (accessed: November 2, 2008)

religions, namely Christianity and Islam. Various interfaith activities have regrettably moved along this direction. This is clear from the Presidential address to the nation by President Olusegun Obasanjo after the Kaduna religious –Sharia crisis of 2000. In his address, as cited by Oranika, he said:

We appreciate the formation and the work of the Inter-Religious Council (NIREC), which has been charged with the responsibility of promoting ideals of peaceful coexistence, especially among the various religions in our country. They have held several meetings, Christians and Moslems, and were in fact under the impression they were making considerable progress, when the upheavals in Kaduna occurred."[4]

We see in the Presidential speech, a conspicuous absence of traditional religion. It was only a dialogue between Christians and Muslims. It is obvious, as the President noted that NIREC were under an illusive impression that considerable progress was being made. Nevertheless, they were proved wrong by the Kaduna crises. The question is: How can one make the desired progress when one is not using the right methodology in addressing a situation. In the South-East also the situation is no different. It has always been a dialogue between Christianity and traditional religion. However, I must credit their efforts and discussions as being aimed at exchanging ideas and opinions towards conflict resolution and fostering harmonious coexistence. Nevertheless, to what extent these objectives have been achieved is questionable. The reason for this failure or minimal result, I believe, lies in the methodology, which is DIALOGUE. In a community with three dominant religions, dialogue, as used in the Nigerian context, excludes one of the three religions. The excluded always feel treated as less significant in the mutual and peaceful existence of the society. As a way of exerting its self-importance, the excluded group not only sabotages the efforts of the other two, it also creates more avenues for conflict and violence. As a lasting solution to the problem of religious violence

---

[4]   Oranika, *One Nation, Two Systems*, 45-46.

and intolerance, without rejecting the word and process of dialogue, so rich in meaning and in the spirit of brotherhood, there is need for the interfaith relationship in Nigeria to advance from dialogue to trialogue.

What is trialogue, one may ask, and why is it effective? The word "trialogue" was not in use until the late 1970s, when it not only appeared but also became popular.[5] Since then trialogue has been defined as, "An interchange and discussion of ideas among three groups having different origins, philosophies, principles, and (doctrines)."[6] This definition and concept clearly explains the model for interfaith relationships, which I am proposing for Nigeria. It means an interchange and discussion of ideas among Christians, Muslims, and followers of African Traditional Religion, who, no doubt, have different origins, beliefs, practices and doctrines. This type of interchange and discussion has clearly been absent in the religious atmosphere of Nigeria in general and the South-East in particular. One very striking element of trialogue is the participation by all three religions in Nigeria without any one of them being relegated to the position of observer. Hence, trialogue is rightly understood as, "A conversation or discussions in which three people or groups participate."[7] We see here a clear difference between the two models of interfaith relationships – dialogue and trialogue. In dialogue within the Nigerian context, the only participants in the North are Christians and Muslims. Followers of Traditional religion only observe from a distance. On other hand, in trialogue they will participate along side with Christians and Muslims. The same applies in the South-East. In dialogue within the South-Eastern context, the only participants are Christians and traditional religionists, the Muslims only observing from afar. In trialogue, the Muslims will

---

[5]   Paul McFedries, Word Spy – Trialogue. http://www.wordspy.com/words/trialogue.asp (accessed: November 11, 2009)

[6]   *Trialogue–Definition at your Dictionary.* http://www.yourdictionary.com/trialogue (accessed: November 11, 2009)

[7]   Dictionary: TrialogueAnswers.com,   http://www.answers.com/trialogue (accessed: November 3, 2008)

participate in the interchange of ideas and conversation or discussion alongside Christians and traditional religionists.

Dialogue within the Nigerian context is exclusive while trialogue is inclusive, that is why, while not completely rejecting dialogue, I am proposing a shift to trialogue in the interfaith relationships among the religions in Nigeria. The reason behind this shift is simple: The goal of interfaith relationships in Nigeria is to build harmonious relationships between all the participating religious communities. In this case, if any one of them is left out along the line of dialogue (involving only two religions, as is the case today), such trust and relationships will not be achieved, and hence the aim of realizing a Nigeria free of religious violence will not be achieved. It is along the line of trialogue (involving all three religions as equal partners) that mutual understanding and harmony can be achieved. Again, a trialogical relationship puts one religion in a position of trust to act as a third party in the event of a conflict involving two other religions. For example, in a conflict involving Christians and ATRs in the South East, Muslim religious leaders can act as a third party in bring peace and harmony among these two religions. Nevertheless, the Muslim leaders can only do this if they have been part of an ongoing trialogical relationship involving them, the Christians and ATR. Already African Traditional Religion has offered a shared foundation: its festivals, as has been demonstrated in the previous chapter, enable Christians, Muslims and ATRs to experience trialogical relationships through celebrations.

1.2. Putting in place programs that encourage and promote interpersonal encounters.

Efforts must be made to put in place programs that encourage interpersonal relationships and encounters. Institutional forms[8] of interfaith relationships, as important as they are, should be less

---

[8]   Institutional forms are the relationships at the level of organized religions and religious leaders, experts, governmental and non-governmental group activities which are aimed at promoting interreligious/interfaith activities.

emphasized. When institutional form is the only available option for interfaith relationships, one should ensure that the institutions involved are not only academically oriented, but are actively involved in designing and promoting programs that will encourages interpersonal encounters. In essence,

> Interfaith relationships should not be restricted to the circles of specialists or visits and committees of religious leaders and politicians. Interfaith relationships must express and include all aspects of life and should be found in every place where Muslims, Christians and [ATR] live and work together, love, suffer and die . . . Besides the various places of interfaith where all are called to share with their brothers and sisters of other religious traditions, there are also favorable times and special events when those who take part are ready to set aside their distinctiveness to have fellowship together in the mutual awareness of common values.[9]

The reason for proffering this guideline for successful interfaith relationships in Nigeria is not far-fetched. For years and decades, interfaith relationships in Nigeria have been institutionalized. The emphasis has been on the Christian Association of Nigeria (CAN) and the Supreme Council of Islamic Affairs in Nigeria. Centered on "leading Imams, Christian leaders and traditional rulers,"[10] this approach has gone from one committee of scholars, political and religious leaders to another. This can be seen in Jan Boer's report on the Kaduna crisis:

> The Kaduna State Government relaxed the curfew from 24 hours to 12, and inaugurated a 5-man judicial commission to investigate this week's two days of rioting by Christian and Muslim youths . . . The commission

---

9   Maurice Borrmans, ed., *Interreligious Document, Vol. I: Guidelines for Dialogue between Christians and Muslims (Pontifical Council for Interreligious Dialogue.)* (New York: Paulist Press, 1990), 29-30.

10   Oranika, *One Nation, Two Systems*, 46.

which has four weeks to conclude its assignment is
under the chairmanship of Justice Ja'afaru Dalhat. Other
members are Alhaji Akilu Idris, Mr. P. Y. Lolo, Mr.
Victor Gwani and Alhaji Tukur Usman. Mr. Dominic
G. Yahaya would serve as secretary, while Mr. Gamaliel
Kure is the commission's counsel.[11]

As we can see, these measures towards lasting peace and mutual
coexistence among the religions are only institutional approaches.
Most of the time, those involved in these institutions, like the leaders
of the Christian Association of Nigeria and the Supreme Council
of Islamic Affairs in Nigeria, leading Imams, Christian leaders,
traditional rulers, and those involved in the commissions and
committees, are rarely a part of the conflict nor are they ever present
at the scene of the violence. Those who are the actual participants,
culprits and victims are left out of these institutional approaches.
Again, even when a committee approach is necessary, appointments
to such committees are politicized. Those who are appointed may
be experts in their various fields of endeavor but are "clueless" about
matters of religion and interfaith activities. This is evident from the
constitution of the commission cited above. The members were,
no doubt, experts and accomplished scholars in the fields of law,
economics, the military, and politics, but were not experts in religious
matters. One can imagine how viable their recommendation will be
towards "pushing the acts of religious violence behind us once and
for all in order to enable us to forge ahead"[12] as stated in their terms
of reference. As mentioned above, expertise in one filed of learning
does not make one an expert in religious conflict resolution. Most
violence has occurred even while such commissions were still
meeting on a previous violent matter or shortly after they submitted
their report. The reason for such re-occurrences could be many, but
include the fact that those who are the actual victims or perpetrators

---

[11]   Jan H. Boer, *Nigeria's Decade of Blood, 1980-2002.* (Ontario
Canada: Essence Publishing, 2003), 120,128.

[12]   Ibid, 128.

are left out of the attempt of finding solutions to violence, and that most of those who are appointed into such commissions do not have the training and commitment to proffer solutions that will bring about lasting peace.

Having carefully observed the ineffectiveness of the institutional approach to religious violence and interfaith relationships among the religions in Nigeria, I am suggesting a change of emphasis and approach: From an institutional approach to an interpersonal and daily life approach, from an academic or committee, approach to a communion and faith sharing approach. In this new approach, true reconciliation, healing, tolerance, and other interfaith activities will begin with the actual victims of religious violence and intolerance. This approach entails a life religious partner: a real person you can keep in touch with, walk along with in the same community and environment, understand and see each other as brothers, sisters, and friends, rather than as members of different religious affiliations. It entails emptying one's cup (being open to learn and to remove one's biases and prejudices against the other). It entails sharing table and meal fellowship while being conscious of the other's dietary laws, and sharing worship fellowship. As observed by the Pontifical Council for Interreligious Dialogue,

> We cannot stress too much of the enormous value of dialogue [trialogue] in circumstances where we eat together, work side by side, endure as in one body the same suffering and enjoy times of celebration with shared pleasure. Through this daily joint experience of the most humble but significant aspects of life Christians and Muslims [and ATR] can help each other to deal with the greatest questions of the world, humanity and God . . . So it is perhaps in this way that believers can improve the quality of their life, articulating their hopes for their fellow humans and their aspiration for God. In a relationship of mutuality they must constantly be

strong enough to call their own lives into question and
to show genuine concern for others.[13]

I unconsciously, without having any interfaith activity in mind,
practiced and promoted this guideline in one of the parishes where I served.
It was a powerful means of witnessing and promoting peace, love, unity
to each other, without spoken words on religious dogmas and doctrines.
In this approach, people realize more consciously, who they are: a people
living together with each other, and committed to the common good of
all. This I believe is far more effective than the institutional approach.

Note that I am not condemning institutional contributions
in religious tolerance and interfaith relationships. Institutions are
important, but not in the way that they have been used in Nigeria.
As observed in the previous chapters, the actual field of violence and
interaction is at the grass roots where people of different religions
relate with and see each other on a daily basis. Effective interfaith
relationships towards mutual co-existence should lay strong emphasis
on interpersonal relationships and put in place programs that will
positively promote such relationships

1.3. Acceptance, respect and recognition of the values of each other.

Interfaith relationships and activity depend on trust and good
relations between individuals, organizations and communities. As
Nigerians and religious people we should show each other respect
and courtesy, especially in our dealings with people of other faiths
and beliefs. This means exercising good will and:

◊ Respecting other people's freedom within the law to express
their beliefs and convictions;

◊ Learning to understand what others actually believe and
value, and letting them express this in their own terms;

◊ Respecting the convictions of others about food, dress
and social etiquette and not behaving in ways which cause
needless offence;

---

[13] Borrmans, *Interreligious Document,* 33.

◊ Recognizing that all of us at times fall short of the ideals of our own traditions and never comparing our own ideals with other people's practices;

◊ Working to prevent disagreement from leading to conflict;

◊ Always seeking to avoid violence in our relationships.

There is no better way to stress the points made in this guideline other than using the words of the Pontifical Council for Interreligious Dialogue and applying them to the Nigerian situation:

> It is time to put an end to an unhappy past of opposition and misunderstanding by following the example of Abraham, who was able to receive guests at the oaks of Mamre, sharing the best he had with them . . . To welcome others in the spirit of Abraham, the 'friend of God,' is more than just the basic sign of politeness or a rite of traditional courtesy. It involves recognition of and respect for others as they are, even in their difference. Hospitality understood thus can never be satisfied with a merely ephemeral kindness. Receiving others decisively into one's experience and taking their distinctive nature into account provide an opportunity for self-renewal and enrichment. To accept one another assumes then that Christians and Muslims [and ATR] recognize each other's profound differences, respect each other in the diversity of their religious traditions and try, in meeting, to find out more about each other. This leads to a growth in mutual esteem and respect. In the name of truth and realism, we must take full account of the specific religious background of our dialogue [trialogue] partners, with all that it involves of intellectual and emotional attachment.[14]

Furthermore, there must be recognition of the values of the other persons' religions. This recognition entails a realization that every religious practice is an attempt, however incomplete it may

---

14   Ibid, 31-32.

be, to exemplify the ideals of their faith.[15] This acceptance, respect and recognition will instill a deeper awareness in the followers of the three religions that others are fully persons capable of mutual understanding. In this, they will together opt to clarify their respective positions in a spirit of interfaith relationships and trialogue, thus transcending the prejudices, bitterness, and misunderstandings that have accumulated on all sides throughout their history in Nigeria.

1.4. Equality of all participants.

Another important guideline, given the Nigerian religious 'ego,' is for all participants in interfaith activities (formal or informal) to understand that none is superior to the other. There should be no host in the strict sense of the word, rather all religions and participants involved are co-hosts. In the words of Ismail Faruqi,

> No dialogue can succeed where one party is "host" and the others are "invited guests." Every party must be host and feel itself so. Every party must feel absolutely free to speak its own mind . . . There can be no "upper hand" and "lower hand" in dialogue; all "hands" must be equal.[16]

This is the view expressed by Vatican II in saying that relationships with people of other faith require that each treats the other or others on an equal footing.[17] For any genuine exchange between different persons to take place, all persons or groups have to have full, free and equal access to the table of dialogue and or trialogue. All must be heard and be taken seriously. As expressed by Gregory Baum, "The conversation involving two or more participants is only fruitful if there is a certain equality of power among them."[18] In another place, Baum stated, "Dialogue demands

---

[15]   Ibid, 45.

[16]   Ismil Rājī al Fārūqī, *Trialogue of the Abrahamic Faiths.* (Maryland: amana publications, 1995), x-xi.

[17]   *Unitatis Redintegratio*, 9.

[18]   Gregory Baum, "The Socio Context of American Catholic Theology." In *Catholic Theology in North American Context: Current*

equality. Honest conversation is not possible between partners that have an unequal access to power."[19] This means countering the tendencies of individuals and faith communities to assume or even to teach that they are inherently superior to others; there should be an equality of all participants. The participants "must rid themselves of all inferiority or superiority complexes, and become ever more receptive of the way those from the other religions explain themselves and their traditions."[20]

This spirit of equality has not been the case in Nigeria. In Nigeria the missionary religions – Islam and Christianity, see themselves as living and transforming religions and claim superiority over each other as the chosen channel for that work of transformation; they both see ATR as a dead and or inferior religion. There are many ways these religions manifest their superior tendencies against each other. For example: a) by stating that they are the 'final' religion –God's last instrument in historical time (e.g. Islam and Christianity), b) by stating that they are the oldest of the religions – God's first revelation and the foundation from which all else has derived (e.g. ATR), c) by stating that they have the monopoly of truth and the only way to salvation (e.g. Muslims and Christians independently), d) by stating that they are the only revealed and incarnate religion (e.g. Christianity), and e) by stating that they allow multiple points of view as part of a basic religious outlook (e.g. ATR).

There is a problem, however, with all the strategies adopted here: the 'finality' of the religion is defined as a function of one tradition only. The fact of being ancient, recent or multiple-minded is not sufficient reason for holding to that 'finality' in today's religiously plural world. 'Finality' turns out to be an ideological construction and not an experiential judgment. We can point out the difficulty in another way. All religions emerge into history as the result of an

---

Issues in Theology (CTSA Proceedings). Ed. George Kilkourse. (Macon: Mercer University Press, 1986), 92.

[19]   Gregory Baum, "Religious pluralism and Common Values." *The Journal of Religious Pluralism,* 4: 1-16

[20]   Borrmans, *Interreligious Document,* 32.

experience of revelation or disclosure of truth. This is what gives a religion a particular cultural shape – religions originate within certain boundaries. Yet the missionary, living and 'transforming' religions extend themselves beyond those early boundaries to claim a universal truth, a truth for all times and places. This type of stance and attitude is a hindrance to sincere and genuine interfaith relationships, and hence must be avoided.

Equality of participants in interfaith activities implies holding one another in high esteem as well as tolerating and accommodating one another. In the words of Simeon Ilesanmi,

> Religious adherents and groups also need to make conscious attempts to cultivate a tolerant attitude towards each other, thereby helping to cerate and sustain a civil environment. Only when people are willing to tolerate each other's existence, the existence of their houses of worship, and the rights of every religious group to proselytize can they experience social peace and, perhaps, material progress as well. The importance of the habit of live and let live goes beyond the lure of moral prudence; it is a theological affirmation of God's presence in every being and every association organized in His name.[21]

To have fruitful interfaith relationships that will bring about peaceful co-existence in Nigeria, all participants must be treated equally. They must be to one another reminders and monitors of equality.

1.5. Inclusive/parallel tendency rather than exclusive tendency.

Inclusivism is a religious theory that accepts that religious truth does not subsist only in one's own religion; other religions also have the truth, even though not its fullness. Parallelism implies that

---

[21] Simeon O. Ilesanmi, *Religious Pluralism and the Nigerian State.* (Ohio: Center for International Studies Ohio University, 1977), 256.

religious truth is found equally in all religions. Therefore, "different religions must be different paths leading to the same goal, just as there are different paths up a mountain leading to the same summit. They (the different religions), just constitute different ways of getting to the same end."[22]

Relations among religions in Nigeria have been extremely exclusive. Each "claims that only those who believe in their 'own way' are true worshippers and are saved."[23] With this tendency, there is no meeting point among these religions because each excludes and condemns the other. Thus, for interfaith relationships to occur in Nigeria, all the religions must move beyond an exclusive tendency to an inclusive tendency that accepts, welcomes and embraces other religions. As expressed by Knitter, "The recognition that our conversation, if it is going to be reasonable and effective, has to be inclusive leads us to the equally important but unsettling recognition that it has been exclusive."[24] In most cases, for examples, Christians and Muslims have always excluded ATR in interfaith discussions and activities.

In terms of their teachings, the religions should adopt an attitude of parallelism that recognizes all religions as authentically seeking and finding God in their ways; and an attitude of interpretation that helps them,

> To realize that our neighbor's religion does not only
> challenge and may even enrich our own, but that
> ultimately, the very differences that separate us are
> somewhat potentially within the world of my own
> religious convictions; to accept that the other religion
> may complement mine and we may even entertain the

---

22 Gary E. Kessler, *Philosophy of Religion: Toward a Global Perspective.* (Belmont, CA: Wadsworth Publishing Company, 1999), 530.

23 Marc Boss, "Religious Diversity: From Tillich to Lindbeck and Back." In *Religion in the New Millennium: Theology in the Spirit of Paul Tillich.* Raymond F. Bulman & Frederick J. Parrella, Eds. (Macon, Georgia: Mercer University Press, 2001), 179.

24 Knitter, *One Earth Many Religions,* 90.

idea that in some particular cases it may well supplement some of my beliefs provided that my religiousness remains an undivided whole . . . The obvious positive aspect of this attitude is the tolerance, broadmindedness and mutual confidence that it inspires. No religion is totally foreign to my own; within our religions, we may encounter the religion of the other; we all need one another.[25]

The search and quest for religious understanding and interfaith relationships is greatly "enriched in the process of interpretation, integration, and mutual appreciation. No human is an island and it is the same with religions. We come to understand ourselves, by understanding others."[26]

1.6. Seek issue based activities and common grounds more on what unites rather than what divides.

In order to have fruitful interfaith relationships in Nigeria that will narrow down the gulf between the three religions, adherents should always emphasize the common teachings of their religion, namely love, peace, good neighborliness and honesty among others. Churches, Mosques, and Shrines should emphasize as well as seek communion in things that build and encourage tolerance, compassion, sharing, charity, solidarity, promote peaceful co-existence, and love; inspiring one and all to choose the path of freedom and responsibility. Religions must be a source of helpful energy. Religious leaders should avoid inflammatory statements particularly in places of worships and in the presence of worshippers.

All participants are to seek issues based activity, for instance, to address poverty and development. It is in this context that dialogue between faith groups and for-profit and non-profit organizations has

---

[25] Raimundo Panikkar, *The Intrareligious Dialogue.* (New York: Paulist Press, 1999), 9.

[26] Kessler, *Philosophy of Religion*, 531.

become necessary. No technical agency and faith community could make changes on a significant scale without making alliances. The faith communities, who often are natural advocates for the poor and have an impressive repository of grassroots experience, can help in eradicating poverty by collaborating with other agencies that have significantly contributed in addressing the issue of poverty and the eradication of diseases in Nigeria. For example, the Multi-national oil companies, the telecommunication giants in Nigeria, and even the World Bank have made developmental efforts and waged war against poverty, malaria and HIV/AIDS in Nigeria to bring about much needed improvement for poor Nigerians. These efforts will yield more dividends when faith communities together align themselves with these agencies. It should be noted that in the previous chapters, poverty was identified as one of the causes of religious violence in Nigeria.

1.7. Being sensitive, honest, straightforward and openhearted.

Participants in interfaith trialogue must do so in a sincere spirit of being sensitive to the teachings and feelings of others. They must be honest, straightforward and openhearted. This implies that they do not approach others with preconceived notions. They should be no ready-made ideas and images including arbitrary judgments and persistent prejudices, if the meeting with others and cooperation with them are to take place according to truth and charity.[27]

When we talk about matters of faith with one another, we need to do so with sensitivity, honesty and straightforwardness. This means:

◊ Recognizing that listening as well as speaking is necessary for a genuine conversation;

◊ Being honest about our beliefs and religious allegiances;

◊ Not misrepresenting or disparaging other people's beliefs and practices;

---

[27] Borrmans, *Interreligious Document,* 70.

◊ Correcting misunderstanding or misrepresentations not only of our own but also of other faiths whenever we come across them;

◊ Being straightforward about our intentions;

◊ Accepting that in formal inter faith meetings there is a particular responsibility to ensure that the religious commitment of all those who are present will be respected. All of us want others to understand and respect our views. Some people will also want to persuade others to join their faith. In a multi faith society where this is permitted, the attempt should always be characterized by self-restraint and a concern for the other's freedom and dignity.

1.8. Recognize and then forgive wrongs of the past.

If ATR, Christians and Muslims were to draw up a list of misunderstandings, hostilities and injustices that have accumulated through the years of their history in Nigeria, they would certainly lose heart, for the long list would contain legitimate accusations and justified grievances put forward in perfectly good faith by both sides.

In a true spirit of interfaith, all concerned should honestly acknowledge a collective responsibility for all the religious violence and conflicts that rocked the nations for decades. This acknowledgment is to lead to the forgiveness of oneself and to the forgiveness of other persons involved in the violence. This point is expressed in the guidelines of the Pontifical Council for Interreligious Dialogue,

> [ATR, Christians and Muslims] should encourage one another to seek, through self-criticism, a more equitable assessment of the tragic events of their common history. Those events should be studied in an atmosphere of mutual consultation and sound historical criticisms, so that, through a joint reinterpretation of them, any

tendentious or even dishonest appeal to religious values
might be avoided. [28]

By dissociating Traditional, Christian, and Muslim religious
values from the injustices of the past which believers have committed
in their name, or which have been falsely attributed to them, it is
possible to imagine a willingness on the part of all concerned to
overlook any remaining ill effects of those injustices. This process of
discernment and forgiveness must continue, for ATR, Christians,
and Muslims. They need to apply it to the historical events of the
present in which they are active participants. Forgiveness within this
context does not mean to forget what had happened in the past, but
drawing from the bitterness of those experiences to let go of past
hurts and pains and resolving to make better things that were done
wrongly in the past.

1.9. Reference the Nigerian Constitution on religious freedom and the UN Declaration on the elimination of all forms of intolerance and discrimination based on religion and belief.

Two major documents that should form a reference point for
interfaith trialogue, relationships and activities among the three
religions in Nigeria are the Nigerian Constitution and the UN
Declaration on issues of religious tolerance. Nigeria is a member
state of the United Nations, and thus should at least nominally
subscribe to this UN declaration.

The section of the Nigeria constitution that deals with religious
freedom and tolerance has been covered in volume one of this series
on Interfaith. We shall now look into to the UN Declaration on the
elimination of all forms of intolerance and discrimination based on
religion and belief. Below is the declaration as given by the United
Nations General Assembly Resolution of 1981:

> *The General Assembly,*
> Considering that one of the basic principles of the
> Charter of the United Nations is that of the dignity

---

[28]   Ibid, 69.

and equality inherent in all human beings, and that all Member States have pledged themselves to take joint and separate action in co-operation with the Organization to promote and encourage universal respect for and observance of human rights and fundamental freedoms for all, without distinction as to race, sex, language or religion,

Considering that the Universal Declaration of Human Rights and the International Covenants on Human Rights proclaim the principles of nondiscrimination and equality before the law and the right to freedom of thought, conscience, religion and belief,

Considering that the disregard and infringement of human rights and fundamental freedoms, in particular of the right to freedom of thought, conscience, religion or whatever belief, have brought, directly or indirectly, wars and great suffering to mankind, especially where they serve as a means of foreign interference in the internal affairs of other States and amount to kindling hatred between peoples and nations,

Considering that religion or belief, for anyone who professes either, is one of the fundamental elements in his conception of life and that freedom of religion or belief should be fully respected and guaranteed,

Considering that it is essential to promote understanding, tolerance and respect in matters relating to freedom of religion and belief and to ensure that the use of religion or belief for ends inconsistent with the Charter of the United Nations, other relevant instruments of the United Nations and the purposes and principles of the present Declaration is inadmissible,

Convinced that freedom of religion and belief should also contribute to the attainment of the goals of world peace, social justice and friendship among peoples and to the elimination of ideologies or practices of colonialism and racial discrimination,

Noting with satisfaction the adoption of several, and the coming into force of some, conventions, under the aegis of the United Nations and of the specialized agencies, for the elimination of various forms of discrimination, Concerned by manifestations of intolerance and by the existence of discrimination in matters of religion or belief still in evidence in some areas of the world, Resolved to adopt all necessary measures for the speedy elimination of such intolerance in all its forms and manifestations and to prevent and combat discrimination on the ground of religion or belief,

Proclaims this Declaration on the Elimination of All Forms of Intolerance and of Discrimination Based on Religion or Belief:

Article 1

1. Everyone shall have the right to freedom of thought, conscience and religion. This right shall include freedom to have a religion or whatever belief of his choice, and freedom, either individually or in community with others and in public or private, to manifest his religion or belief in worship, observance, practices and teaching.

2. No one shall be subject to coercion, which would impair his freedom to have a religion or belief of his choice.

3. Freedom to manifest one's religion or belief may be subject only to such limitations as are prescribed by law and are necessary to protect public safety, order, health or morals or the fundamental rights and freedoms of others.

Article 2

1. No one shall be subject to discrimination by any State, institution, group of persons, or person on the grounds of religion or other belief.

2. For the purposes of the present Declaration, the expression "intolerance and discrimination based on religion or belief" means any distinction, exclusion,

restriction or preference based on religion or belief and having as its purpose or as its effect nullification or impairment of the recognition, enjoyment or exercise of human rights and fundamental freedoms on an equal basis.

Article 3

Discrimination between human being on the grounds of religion or belief constitutes an affront to human dignity and a disavowal of the principles of the Charter of the United Nations, and shall be condemned as a violation of the human rights and fundamental freedoms proclaimed in the Universal Declaration of Human Rights and enunciated in detail in the International Covenants on Human Rights, and as an obstacle to friendly and peaceful relations between nations.

Article 4

1. All States shall take effective measures to prevent and eliminate discrimination on the grounds of religion or belief in the recognition, exercise and enjoyment of human rights and fundamental freedoms in all fields of civil, economic, political, social and cultural life.

2. All States shall make all efforts to enact or rescind legislation where necessary to prohibit any such discrimination, and to take all appropriate measures to combat intolerance on the grounds of religion or other beliefs in this matter.

Article 5

1. The parents or, as the case may be, the legal guardians of the child have the right to organize the life within the family in accordance with their religion or belief and bearing in mind the moral education in which they believe the child should be brought up.

2. Every child shall enjoy the right to have access to education in the matter of religion or belief in accordance with the wishes of his parents or, as the case may be, legal guardians, and shall not be compelled to receive

teaching on religion or belief against the wishes of his parents or legal guardians, the best interests of the child being the guiding principle.

3. The child shall be protected from any form of discrimination on the ground of religion or belief. He shall be brought up in a spirit of understanding, tolerance, friendship among peoples, peace and universal brotherhood, respect for freedom of religion or belief of others, and in full consciousness that his energy and talents should be devoted to the service of his fellow men.

4. In the case of a child who is not under the care either of his parents or of legal guardians, due account shall be taken of their expressed wishes or of any other proof of their wishes in the matter of religion or belief, the best interests of the child being the guiding principle.

5. Practices of a religion or belief in which a child is brought up must not be injurious to his physical or mental health or to his full development, taking into account article 1, paragraph 3, of the present Declaration.

Article 6
In accordance with article I of the present Declaration, and subject to the provisions of article 1, paragraph 3, the right to freedom of thought, conscience, religion or belief shall include, inter alia, the following freedoms:

(a) To worship or assemble in connection with a religion or belief, and to establish and maintain places for these purposes;

(b) To establish and maintain appropriate charitable or humanitarian institutions;

(c) To make, acquire and use to an adequate extent the necessary articles and materials related to the rites or customs of a religion or belief;

(d) To write, issue and disseminate relevant publications in these areas;

(e) To teach a religion or belief in places suitable for these purposes;

(f) To solicit and receive voluntary financial and other contributions from individuals and institutions;

(g) To train, appoint, elect or designate by succession appropriate leaders called for by the requirements and standards of any religion or belief;

(h) To observe days of rest and to celebrate holidays and ceremonies in accordance with the precepts of one's religion or belief; i.) To establish and maintain communications with individuals and communities in matters of religion and belief at the national and international levels.

Article 7

The rights and freedoms set forth in the present Declaration shall be accorded in national legislation in such a manner that everyone shall be able to avail himself of such rights and freedoms in practice.

Article 8

Nothing in the present Declaration shall be construed as restricting or derogating from any right defined in the Universal Declaration of Human Rights and the International Covenants on Human Rights.[29]

If the three religions in Nigeria adhere to all the above guidelines, interfaith relationships and activities will bear successful fruits for lasting peace, harmony and stability among the religions and the entire nation.

---

[29]   The United Nations: Declaration on the Elimination of all form of Intolerance and of Discrimination based in Religion or Belief, G.A. res. 36/55,36 U.N. GAOR Supp. (No. 51) at 171, U.N. Doc. A/36/684 (1981).

CHAPTER TWO

COMMITMENT TO INTERFAITH
RELATIONSHIPS IN NIGERIA.

Before engaging in any form of interfaith activities, there be must a commitment that comes from the heart of all those concerned. This commitment acknowledges that the journey of interfaith in not as simple as it may appear to be; but despite the difficulties and diversities that may go with it, all concerned agree and commit themselves to work together. This section will begin with some verbal commitments that are necessary for the interactions among the faith communities in Nigeria. These verbal commitments are necessary because in the course of this research it was discovered that all the religions in Nigeria have been accusing each of having a hidden agenda when calling for any form of relationships. Again, there have been some elements of mistrust regarding the others' intentions. Making verbal commitments in the presence of all participants will help to eliminate suspicion regarding the intentions of one another in coming together for interfaith discussions and activities. It will foster trust among participants.

In order to have fruitful and successful interfaith activities in Nigeria, the followers of the three religions should make the following commitments:

 I. Commitment to be at peace with one another; strive to achieve inner peace through personal reflection and spiritual growth, and to cultivate a spirituality, which manifests itself in action. This is important because most attempts to bring religious followers in Nigeria together have ended in anything but peacefulness. In addition, the religious atmosphere in the country most often has been very tense as observed in chapter six of this work. In this situation, a commitment to peace with one another is essential.

II. Commitment to support and strengthen the home and family as the nursery of peace. Again, as observed in chapter seven and eight of this work, most families have ATR, Muslims and Christians living under the same roof. The practical lesson of peace they give to themselves and their children is a seed and lesson for peace in the larger community and nation.

III. Commitment to resolve or transform conflicts without using violence, and to prevent them through education and the pursuit of justice.

IV. Commitment to underline the importance of understanding, tolerance and respect for religious, non-religious and cultural diversity as integral for our well-being, stability, prosperity and peace and a determination to fulfill our responsibility to contribute to global efforts in promoting interfaith and intercultural understanding. Also to reject stereotyping and the use of violence in the name of religions, faiths or ideologies, and to oppose extremism. This commitment is important because in the course of this research it was observed that most violence in Nigeria is a result of lack of understanding and or respect of the others' religious values. Violence has also been fueled by misinformation and stereotypes that paint the other religion as an enemy that must be resisted at all cost.

V. Commitment to work towards a reduction of the scandalous economic differences between human groups and other forms of violence and threats to peace, such as waste of resources, extreme poverty, racism, all types of terrorism, lack of caring, corruption, and crime.

VI. Commitment to overcome all forms of discrimination, exploitation, and domination and to promote institutions based on shared responsibility and participation. Human rights, including religious freedom and the rights of minorities, must be respected. This commitment is important because in some parts of Nigeria, some religions, as observed in chapter six, have created the impression that no other religions except theirs can be practiced in that part of the country. Again, that you can only get a job if you belong to a certain religion. This commitment will give all the participants the trust and confidence that all parts of Nigeria are open and free for all religions to exist.

VII. Commitment to provide opportunities for conversation, partnership, education, hospitality, and shared celebrations. Emphasis on education for peace, freedom, and human rights, and religious education to promote openness and tolerance is a necessity. Ignorance has been one of the fundamental reasons for religious violence in Nigeria. This commitment is important because it will advance religious literacy all over Nigeria by abolishing the present system whereby Christian religious knowledge / ATR are not taught in elementary and secondary schools in most Northern (Muslim dominated) states, and Islam / ATR are not taught in most Southern (Christian dominated) states in Nigeria, as observed in the course of this research.

VIII. Commitment to create a friendly environment and pursue common goals that build unity among the religious communities and the nation. Unity and Faith, Peace and Progress is the Motto of the Federal Republic of Nigeria, as written in bold on the Nigerian Coat of Arm. Nevertheless, religious violence seems to have undermined the unity, peace and progress that all Nigerians should enjoy irrespective of their tribal, ethnic or religious affiliations. This commitment aims at rebuilding trust and relationships that will restore confidence in the unity and peace of Nigeria irrespective of religious affiliations.

IX. A renewed commitment to deepening and broadening Interfaith Trialogue for the benefit of a peaceful and fruitful ATR-Muslim-Christian relationship that underscores the importance of consolidating the Interfaith Trialogue as an annual event. This commitment is occasioned by the need to involve all religions along the path of trialogue, where no religion is left out no matter its population, as has been the case in the past.

X. Acknowledgment that in every religion is found admonitions to love and peace, and rejection of hatred and violence, and a set of common universal values that are shared by all religions. This commitment is a realization that the good that exists in one's own religion equally exists in the religions of others; that all religions have something positive to offer in the spirit of interfaith relationships. This will promote the religious equality that some religions tend to deny others in Nigerian society.

XI. Commitment to provide moral leadership to the nations, especially on mutually agreed issues. In Nigeria, religion is generally looked upon as a conscience for the society, but in most cases, as seen in the previous chapters, religions and their leaders have failed the nation in this regard. This commitment therefore aims at repositioning all the religions and their leadership in their moral roles in Nigeria.

XII. Commitment to recognize that God is at work in other religious systems outside and different from our own. We must realize that God is too big to be reduced and tied down within the confines and modes of one religious system.

XIII. Commitment and willingness to always ask this question honestly: is there something that we can learn from the others that will benefit our own spirit, religion and life in general? We must realize that no matter how "infallible" and "holy" we may think our religion is, we humans who practice the religion are fallible and full of imperfections.

Hence, we must be open to learn from each other to correct our own mistakes.

With these commitments in mind, we shall now discuss various forms of interfaith activities in Nigeria.

CHAPTER THREE

ACTIVITIES FOR INTERFAITH RELATIONSHIPS IN NIGERIA

The activities that we shall discuss here are thought experiments and suggestions based on my research of the three religions in Nigeria and on my fieldwork and participation in interfaith activities.

It should be borne in mind that interfaith activity is not a debate, but rather an opportunity to interact, listen and share with each other the foundations of what is important for each religious traditions while learning to understand the common elements inherent in each religion. The purpose is to create a platform on which people can freely meet to get to know each other, providing a forum to celebrate and honor the diversity of our religious beliefs, take common steps to work for peace and harmony among each other, and to take action together on issues of common concern and social needs in the country. The following are activities that will advance these objectives.

3.1. Grassroots activities: Trialogue of life and action.

A trilogue of life is one that occurs in various Nigerian communities where followers of African Traditional Religion live side-by-side with Christians and Muslims. This can be described as informal unstructured encounters and relationships where ordinary adherents of the different religions engage in very useful sharing of experiences and collaborations in life.

This form of interfaith activities is particularly important in Nigeria given the fact that religious pluralism cuts across national, tribal, and at times even family lines. In Nigeria people belonging to different faiths (ATR, Islam, and Christianity) live in the same village, town, or in the same compounds or bloc of flats in the urban areas and even in the same family. They meet at family meetings, births, and marriages and funerals. They work side by side in the same offices, schools, factories, so that a situation for trialogical and interfaith relationships invariably imposes itself on the people who find themselves in such situations. Without directly discussing matters of religions, they share their human experiences: talking about their children, the brotherhood that binds them together, common national, tribal and community needs, their jobs, and their basic economic necessities. Here the central topic of discussion is not religion. Rather believers live out what their religions have taught them about good neighborliness, about honesty, dedication to duty, justice, service to one another, love, duties in the family, and community development. Taking, for example, my own community where Christians and ATR live as neighbors, a Christian going to the farm or to the market can entrust the care of his or her children to the care of a follower of ATR without fear of religious indoctrination or any physical harm. Again, a bereaved Christian family and vice versa is consoled by members of other religions, offering the material and spiritual support that such a person requires at such trying moments. If need be, they can draw from the teachings of each other to console one another on the necessity of death and the hope in the after-life.

3.2. Trialogue of action: Community partnership building.

Besides the trialogue of life, another form of interfaith activity needed in the Nigerian society is the trialogue of action that calls together and challenges all the religions in Nigeria to work together in community partnerships. This activity aims at addressing common concerns and needs in society. Faith-based organizations can contribute to achieving the Vision 2020 Development Goals of Nigeria[30] by drawing on their social capital in terms of people's trust, religious and humanitarian motivation, and solidarity with one's neighbor in need, regardless of his/her faith and conviction. They are in a special position to reach out to the poorest members in the community and to mobilize needed resources at all levels. Faith-based organizations can also provide the governments at national and local levels with an integral framework that goes beyond material benefits and encompasses, amongst others, the spiritual dimension. Through concrete actions many-faith based organizations and religious leaders (male and female)—in cooperation with governments, other civil society groups and businesses—also help address immediate needs of people. They also provide the elements for sustainable development through values formation and empowerment.

Working together in community projects and engaging in community service activities together is an excellent way to bridge the misunderstandings that exist between religious communities and at the same time offer service to the community. Such areas of community service include health care, education, poverty eradication, and collaborating with government in the provision of basic infrastructures and other amenities lacking in most Nigerian communities. As observed by Illesanmi,

> Several studies have shown the important role of religious institutions in the fields of health and education in Nigeria. To be sure, schools and hospitals were initially used by their proprietors for proselytizing and missionary purposes. But they also provided at least a modicum of spiritual and symbolic cohesion for the social order.[31]

---

[30] Vision 2020 development goal for Nigeria is a goal set by the government aiming that by year 2020 Nigeria will be one of the 20 largest economies in the world, able to consolidate its leadership role in Africa and establish itself as a significant player in the global economic and political arena.

[31] Ilesanmi, *Religious Pluralism and the Nigerian State*, 237.

Joint projects have great potential to deepen understanding between participants: working side by side gives people a real chance to get to know each other and develop relationships of trust. These can be very simple projects, like coming together to improve a deserted piece of land or paint a community centre, or more complex ones like joint faith community initiatives to respond to the needs of refugees or provide help for the homeless or to work to help people overcome drug addiction. There is already an initiative by Christians and Muslim in Nigeria to work together for the common good under the umbrella of Nigerian Inter-Faith Action Association (NIFAA), an association that was inaugurated on November 11, 2009 in Abuja. The Sultan of Sokoto, Alhaji Mohammed Saad Abubakar III, made the inaugural speech at the ceremony. Reporting on the Sultan's speech, Gbola Subair said,

> NIFAA was set up to address issues such as malaria, HIV and poverty, generally. He [the Sultan] said the association was funded both locally and internationally. He assured Nigerians that the two of them (Alhaji Mohammed Saad Abubakar and Archbishop John Onaiyekan, co-chair of the inaugural ceremony), being moral leaders, would be transparent in running it.[32]

Speaking on the occasion, Onaiyekan described the collaboration between Muslims and Christians as the best thing that has happened to the country.[33]

One problem in this initiative is the exclusion of ATR in such collaboration. This has been the trend of interfaith relationships in Nigeria – a dialogue with two religions and not a trialogue involving the three religions without excluding any. This dissertation is advocating for more inclusive trialogical interfaith activity that will of necessity include all three religions in Nigeria. This is important because such inclusion excludes the spirit of envy, jealousy and

---

[32] Gbola Subair, "Religious Crisis is Sheer Madness, says Sultan." *Nigerian Tribune*, Abuja, November 12, 2009.

[33] Ibid.

bigotry on the part of the followers of the excluded religion. Again, it advances the pace of development. When three competent people undertake a project hitherto left only to two people, the pace of development is faster in terms of human, financial and intellectual resources. Moreover, all the three religions have all it takes – moral standing, commitment for peace and development, and integrity – to partner together in community building and development.

Working together as one in addressing the common needs and concerns of the nation and communities helps promote a culture of peace as a precondition for anti-poverty measures to take place, and has the capability of creating shared spaces that will provide opportunities for all the religions to come together, work together and share many things in common in a spirit of brotherhood, friendship and fellowship. Such shared spaces include, but are not limited to: sacred buildings, neutral rooms within faith buildings, shared and mutual spaces, church halls, community centers, civic and secular spaces – town halls, civic centers, sports centers and leisure facilities, personal spaces such as homes and gardens, enclosed environments that encourage dialogue and sharing experiences. According to Hazel Blears,

> Well managed shared spaces are important in encouraging interaction and in creating opportunities for people to pursue shared activities. Being in the same physical or virtual space is an essential ingredient for meaningful interaction and we know that one of the key factors in successful spaces is that they are safe. Safe spaces are not just places which are secure from physical risk but spaces that have an environment or ethos which allows people to be themselves and to be honest yet respectful, be comfortable but not complacent, be constructive in recognizing difference, be open to sharing concerns and values and help people to move out of their "comfort zone" when, and if, they are ready to do so.[34]

---

[34] Hazel Blears, ed., *Faces to Face and Side by Side: A framework for partnership in our multi-faith Society.* (London: Communities and

With thousands of places of worship in Nigeria, faith communities are essential providers of sacred and secular spaces for people to interact and pursue shared activities. These spaces are found in all parts of our communities from large cities to small rural villages. They are used by local people for local events and activities and often function as the primary resources and buildings for community spaces and essential meeting places.

3.3. Structured interfaith encounters and activities.

This form of interfaith activity is one that is strictly structured around purely religious issues that provide opportunities for interfaith relationships and encounters through meetings, conferences and congresses of religious bodies, faith communities, and faith linked organizations like Organization of Traditional Religions of Africa (OTRA), Supreme Council of Islamic Affairs (SCIA), and Christian Association of Nigeria (CAN). It can be organized at the national, zonal, state, and local community levels. It could take place weekly, monthly, bi-monthly, or at most quarterly; the more the frequency the better the religious harmony and understanding of each other's religions. It would also further bonding among participants. Such meetings, conferences, and congresses could last from one day to at most a week, depending on the nature of the activities being planned.

Below are sample activities for this form of interfaith relationships:

3.3.1. A Day of Prayer:

Various communities and towns can set up a particularly day where all sons and daughters come together to pray for the peace, harmony and progress of their land and community. During this activity, a representative of each religion is given a time to pray in the manner of his/her religion. Nigerians are very religious and spiritual people, hence such a day of inclusive prayer would go a

---

Local Government Publication, 2008), 48-49.

long way to boost relationships among all the religions involved. This activity can occur monthly or quarterly.

3.3.2. Weekly Meditations:

Followers of different religions who are living within the same neighborhood can converge once every week at a chosen time, preferably in the evening when all the day's work is finished. They would gather in one of the member's home (to be rotated among all the participants) to share faith stories from different religious backgrounds (participants can speak about the prayers, ceremonies, rituals, and special celebrations that are part of their religious traditions), pray together, discuss common issues affecting their neighborhood, and share table fellowship while respecting others dietary rules. This is an effective means of community mobilization

3.3.3. Week of Interfaith Relationships:

One week (or at least 3 to 5 days) is to be set aside monthly, bi-monthly or quarterly for interfaith gatherings and relationships by each community, city, state, and zone or national faith-based organization. It could be a weekend (Friday – Sunday) activity. A number of people from across the religions would be delegated (each by his own religious group) to plan the activities for the week. Effort would be made at the planning stage to build relationships with local media. Invite them at least at the opening and closing events, if it is impossible to have them all days because of the cost implications. Publicize success stories through the local media to build confidence within communities and show the benefits of collaborative action. Oftentimes the media only brings to the public the conflict and ugly side of religion. The presence of the media will enable a wider audience to be aware of the interfaith peace and harmonious initiative of the different religious bodies in Nigeria.

Activities for this week may include the following:

1. Acknowledgment of all the participants and their religious affiliations: It gives a sense of courage and brotherhood to

notice that people of other faith are sitting beside you as friends and not as foes.

2. Interfaith worship: The event will begin with an interfaith worship in a selected religious place of worship within the city or in a common ground/shared space. This type of worship demonstrates in practical term that though faiths, tribes and tongues may differ, in brotherhood and under one God we stand. In this activity, members of each faith in turn offer prayers, readings or devotional songs—perhaps in alphabetical or historical order of the religions. Prayers specific to a particular tradition are offered in the presence of people of other faiths.

3. City-Wide rally: People should see ATR, Christians and Muslims dancing and rallying together in the same city with the same message of calling all to live in harmony and peace. This is a very successful means of creating public awareness on the importance of living and working together as one; religious diversity not withstanding.

4. Paper presentations and responses: Topics that touch on the need for religious peace, harmony, and interfaith relationships are to be presented. Presenters are drawn from different religions. Topics may include:

   ◊ Building good relations with people of different faiths and beliefs (This topic is suggested as the first topic because it is a focused starting place to enable participants to move into the general topic of the day/week).

   ◊ Common religious values: What are the values and ethical foundations that are common to all religions? A discussion could encompass how these values, as well as history, beliefs and practices could be understood and appreciated by others while at the same time respecting the integrity of each religious tradition.

   ◊ How does religion contribute or respond to violence?

◊ How can we better live together as part of the human community? What are the joint approaches and common actions religious communities can take in such matters as the environment, social services, and human rights?

◊ The role of African Traditional Religious education in peace and social development in contemporary Nigeria.

◊ Christian education for peace in Nigeria.

◊ Islamic perspectives for a culture of peace in Nigeria

◊ Interreligious conflicts as a threat for peace and national development.

5. Drama/play presentations: Besides paper presentations, drama presentations on interfaith themes and the evil of violence can be presented. This form of presentation serves as a teaching/learning tool and as a recreational tool for participants.

6. Workshops/Discussions: Participants are to break into workshops in the course of the weekly event. The number of times these workshops could occur depends on the number of days for the entire activities. Workshops are chances for general discussions on the types of projects that can help increase interfaith understanding and co-operation. They are chances to look at some of the challenges in making interfaith projects work. The workshops are primarily about participants having an opportunity for genuine discussion and encounter. They are places for mutual learning and for exploring ideas in an open environment.

7. Visitations of religious places of worships: If possible and as time permits, it is important that activities for this week include visiting places of worship of the three religions in Nigeria. (If it is impossible to pay this visit within the week, at least participants are to be encouraged to do so on their own time.) I suggest that followers of ATR and Christianity visit mosques with an Imam to guide their visit, Muslims and

Christians are to visit traditional shrines with a Chief Priest to guide them, while ATR and Muslims visit churches with a clergy to guide them. At the end of such visits, let each group recall either their experiences of African Traditional Religion, Islam, or Christianity, in terms of personal visits to shrines, mosques, and churches, witnessing a prayer session of that particular religion, conversation with someone in such places of worship or any suitable experience. Let them share these with the group.

8. Interfaith prayer session of healing, forgiveness, peace and progress: This is a very vital way of incorporating a real spiritual dimension in the week of interfaith activity. After having listened to and participated in presentations and discussions, participants could admit their own personal and collective contributions to religious intolerance, discrimination, conflicts and violence. They are moved to pray for forgiveness, healing, reconciliation, peace and progress in the land.

9. Resolutions/communiqué: At the end, participants are to come up with resolutions and commitments to live, work and journey together as one for a better religious atmosphere and a peaceful Nigeria. Participant makes these resolutions available to their religious groups and faith-based organizations that they represent at the week of interfaith activity.

10. Closing ceremony: As the ceremony began with a public interfaith worship in a particular religious place of worship, so it should end, but now in another religious place of worship. The event should wind-up with a sumptuous celebration love feast.

3.3.4. Trialogue of experts and example of religious leaders.

This form of interfaith activity refers to learned members from different religions discussing religious issues. A Trialogue of religious experts is a bid to enrich, deepen and clarify their various religious legacies and to appreciate the spiritual values of each other. For this to happen, the experts should be conversant with their own religion and it best happens in a pluralistic society where there is tolerance of and contact between different religions. In this form of activity, religious leaders, in most cases alongside decision makers, be they academic or political, are to come together in a conference, symposium or even at an interpersonal note to discuss some theological and doctrinal issues of their religions, not with a view of winning the argument nor of conversion, but to better understanding some of the why, what and how of the religions of the others.

Chinua Achebe in *Things Fall Apart* gave a good example of an interfaith discussion of experts involving Mr. Brown, a Christian missionary in Igboland and Ichie Akunna, one of the great men and traditionalists of Umuofia village. As narrated by Achebe, Mr. Brown had earlier presumed that the followers of ATR worship Idols made of wood. But through a non-confrontational discussions and clarifications by Ichie Akunna on the ATR's concept of God and divinity, Mr. Brown later came to realize how wrong he was and he as well as his followers began to appreciate and respect ATR in Umuofia village. This example and discussion between the two experts/leaders went a long way to change the hostile attitude that followers of these religions were having for each other.[35]

Besides theological and dogmatic discussions, the example of religious leaders coming together and sitting together is a powerful witness of interfaith relationships to their followers. Nigerians of all works of life rely so much on their religious leaders for guidance, not only in religious and spiritual matters, but also in also political and social issues.

The ability and disposition of religious leaders to respect the cherished traditions of each other, and the spirit to foresee that their actions, as leaders, could positively or negatively affect the promotion of peaceful existence in Nigeria, are very important. This aspect of leadership is what I consider as one of the weaknesses of

---

[35] Chinua Achebe, *Things Fall Apart*. (New York: Anchor Books, 1959), 178-181.

Nigerian religious leaders – ATR, Christians and Muslims – whose actions, utterances and irreverence to the religious sentiments of the other have promoted violence instead of meaningful trialogue and interfaith in Nigeria. Respect toward the persons of the religions' founders is necessary for dialogue. A Muslim cannot willingly enter into trialogue with a Christian or ATR who sees the Prophet Muhammad (Peace be upon him) as the Anti-Christ or instrument of Satan nor will a Christian enter into trialogue with someone who has no respect for the person of Christ. In like manner, ATR will not enter into meaningful trialogue with those who disdain the ancestors. Religious leaders and experts of these religions have a duty of redirecting and educating each other and their followers on the values of each other's traditions. This type of redirection and education will most effectively occur within the environment and climate of interfaith relationships.

3.3.5. Youths for God and for peace programs.

This form of interfaith activity is for the youths, by the youths and with the youths. Although the youths are involved in all the discussed activities, there is the need for an activity that will more actively involve the youth alone. The youths have been at the forefront of religious violence, conflicts and riots that have taken place in Nigeria. They are readymade instruments of violence in the hands of religious and political leaders. Sometimes they make themselves available because of poverty, misinformation, manipulation and unguided religious zeal. As reported by Ayegba Ejibe,

> The Sultan of Sokoto, Alhaji Muhamad Sa'ad Abubakar, while speaking, said without peace, there could not be development. He said the youths must be given requisite training on inter-faith matters towards the common destiny of moving Nigeria forward. The President of the Christian Association of Nigeria (CAN), Arch-Bishop Onaiyekan, said the youth were the most vulnerable when there are incidents of religious crises, saying the

hope of a progressive future for Nigeria has to do with crises free Nigeria.[36]

For religious violence and riots to permanently stop in Nigeria, Nigerian youths must say no to violence, and yes to God and peace. To achieve this yes, we must initiate what I call Youth for God and peace interfaith programs. Already plans are being developed by the Nigerian Inter Religious Council (NIREC) to train 250 youths on how to overcome the issue of religious crisis in Nigeria that has led to the loss of so many lives. The national coordinator, Professor Ishaq Oloyede, disclosed that 50 youths would be selected from Niger State, adding that 25 Christians and Muslims youths would make up the number and the remaining 200 would be split between the two religions based on 100 youths each.[37] This type of training is a step in the right direction, but it is obviously deficient. It conspicuously excludes ATR in such training. Again, it is one thing to undergo training and another to put it into practice in interfaith forums. What we need in Nigeria is an all-inclusive program focusing not only on academia but also on rural and uneducated youth, who seem to be the most vulnerable. Such programs will target the youths in schools at rural and urban communities, and even jobless youths. The following are possible examples of such programs:

3.3.5.1 Encountering Faith.

This refers to the family of activities through which young people explore faith as it is lived and experienced in today's society. Encountering faith aims to build relationships among young people from different religious traditions by empowering them to work together to serve others. It seeks to help young people explore such questions as: How do young people in countries with multi-religious populations express their faith? In what contexts do we encounter faith in our daily lives? What is the relationship between faith and

---

36 Ayegba Israel Ebije, "Nirec Moves to Stop Religious Crisis in the Country." *Daily Trust*. January 23, 2009.
37 Ibid.

political engagement? What is the role of interfaith relationships in our society, and how should they be done?

In addressing these questions, the following activities are employed:

1. Faith stories from the youths' perspective: This involves a range of activities/discussion questions through which young people consider why interfaith dialogue is important and how it should be done. It should also include the telling of a personal story of faith that has a connection with people of the faith. Such a story could be one's involvement in a riot that took many lives out of ignorance or misinformation and the impact such violence made in his/her life that made him/her have a rethink and work for peace instead of violence.

2. The Who? What? When? Where? Why? of interfaith relationships: This implies having a fun activity to discover what interfaith relationships are, who engages in them, when, where, in what ways and, perhaps most importantly, why.

3. The Gallery of Faith Today: An interactive mobile game that leads to a discussion about perceptions about faith, the role of faith in society and the roots of prejudice.

4. Faith & Politics: A group of activities, which explore the complex relationship between faith and politics in Nigerian society today.

5. Learning how to disagree: Activities exploring the art of disagreeing respectfully, from asking sensitively worded questions, to understanding the impact of religious bickering, body language and tone of speech in a discussion.

3.3.5.2. Interfaith fellowship/studies.

This form activity is suitable mainly in such multi-faith environments as schools, youth groups and universities. It is suggested here because most acts of religious violence in Nigeria have occurred in institutions of learning. Using religious texts as the foundation for discussion, students can discuss and investigate the ethical, practical and civic implications of living in a multi-faith society. They can reflect on their own beliefs and roles within the communities, and develop a respect for difference wherever it may occur.

Students can invite each other to worship in their faith community. Members of one faith may invite guests of one or more other faiths to attend their usual act of worship. The guests' presence may be acknowledged just by a special greeting, or a visitor may be asked to read from his or her scriptures, say a prayer or perhaps speak. Christians, for example, might choose hymns centered on God rather than on Christ to make it easier for ATR and Muslims to participate.

Youths in schools can converge and interact at social functions like birthdays, graduations, and end of year parties. These are occasions of coming together and building better understanding.

3.3.5.3. Community service.

Youth community services have an important role to play in building the skills and confidence of young people to link with others from different backgrounds. Young people of faith have a particular role to play in the vision of making Nigeria better through a common action of addressing social ills of injustices, religious and civil conflict, poverty, corruption and underdevelopment. As change-makers for future generations, they are able to establish new forms of inter-faith collaboration by placing a committed concern for the poorest at the heart of a renewed trialogue of life and action.

As kids, one of the community services we used to perform was the sweeping of the community square. All concerned – ATR and Christians – were committed in this service. It was such a moment of interaction and joyful camaraderie. Many events can bring youth together. Various youth groups in different communities should identify activities peculiar to them that will bring them together.

CHAPTER FOUR

OBSTACLES TO INTERFAITH RELATIONSHIPS.

As observed by the Pontifical Council for Inter-religious Dialogue in its document *Dialogue and Proclamation*, relationships on a purely human level are not easy to practice, hence interreligious or interfaith relationship are even more difficult. Consequently, it is important to be aware of the obstacles, which may arise. Some would apply equally to the members of all religious traditions and impede the success of trialogue and interaction. Others may affect some religious traditions more specifically and make it difficult for a process of dialogue/trialogue to be initiated.[38]

Among these obstacles are:

4.1. Insufficient knowledge and understanding of one's own religion or faith.

This lack of knowledge of one's own religion can make dialogue with others frustrating and limit it to the emotional level. The most important thing in interfaith relationships is sharing one's faith, but how can one share what one is not sufficiently grounded in or even ignorant about?

4.2. Lack of sufficient knowledge of other religions.

---

[38] Pontifical Council for Inter-religious Dialogue. *Dialogue and Proclamation*. (Rome: Vatican Press, 1991), n. 51.

Lack of sufficient knowledge and understanding of the belief and practices of other religions, leading to a lack of appreciation for their significance and even at times to misrepresentation, can seriously hinder interfaith dialogue and trialogue. Fundamentalism which is at the root of religious persecution and violence that is so prevalent in our days is caused by this insufficient knowledge and understanding.[39]

4.3. Walls of prejudice.

One of the greatest obstacles to interfaith relationships in Nigeria is the wall of prejudice, which separates the Christians and Muslims from one another and together from ATR. Missionary catechesis for decades has taught the Nigerian converts to hold ATR in great disdain and its adherents in great contempt. This is very evident in the number of derogatory terms and appellations used for ATR and its devotees. Nigerian Christians and Muslims today still refer to ATR as paganism, animism, fetishism, idolatry, and heathenism. Its adherents are correspondingly called pagans, animists, heathens, and idol worshippers. Christians and Muslims still sustain their polemics that it is stupid to be an adherent of ATR, which they see as the citadel of Satan, and disdainfully call its ministers Juju priests, fetish priests, witchdoctors, and agents of the devil. Christians and Muslims in Nigeria having anchored themselves on modern European and Arabic cultures respectively, have engendered in their adherents a superiority complex, which sees ATR and the African cultural values which it upholds as primitive and unprogressive.

4.4. Wrongs and burdens of the past.

So many lives and properties have been lost over the years to religious riots and conflicts in Nigeria that even if all the religions collectively agree to forget and forgive the wrongs of past, there will still be individual followers of these religions who will never see any reason to associate and interact with members of a religion that rendered them homeless and/or orphaned. Obviously, the wrong of

---

[39]   *Dialogue and Proclamation*, 52.

the past will still present certain practical difficulties in the ways of coming together in mutual understanding. It would be illusory to ignore these in an effort to practice interfaith collaborations.

4.5. Exclusivist tendency.

Another real obstacle to religious peaceful coexistence and cooperation comes too often not from the believers' claim of having the truth, but rather from their approach to this conviction. There are believers who believe that no element of truth is found in any other religion other than theirs. This belief leads to exclusivist tendency. An approach that becomes exclusive in terms of relations may even resort to some kind of force and violence in order to fight, submit or exclude those who do not embrace the same truth.

Some scriptural passages strengthen exclusive tendencies among followers. For example, certain Christian scriptures seem to have prevented some Christians from engaging in genuine inter-religious dialogue/trialogue. Some scriptures that can be interpreted in exclusive terms as soteriological fundamentalism can prevent genuine inter-religious trialogue. For instance, the Christian assertion of Jesus Christ as the 'only' way to God stands out as an obstacle: "I am the way and the truth and the life. No one comes to the Father except through me" (John 14:6). Certain conservative Christians can use this exclusive Biblical periscope taken out of its original socio-historical and religious contexts to prevent people from engaging in genuine dialogue with people of non-Christian faiths. Most moderate Christians agree that John 14:6 and its exclusive interpretation have been traditionally used in Christian communities in pluralistic societies to prevent relationships with other faiths.

4.6. Self-sufficiency and lack of openness.

Self-sufficiency and lack of openness leading to defensive or aggressive attitudes can also be an obstacle to dialogue. If, for instance, Christians say 'Christ is the fullness of salvation,' they should not state that they publically and rigidly attach themselves to this statement. We have also said that 'there are seeds of Truth in other religions and cultures' and such a statement is a good attitude towards inter-religious dialogue. Other statements, such as 'Outside the Church, there is no salvation', wrongly interpreted, can be an obstacle to dialogue.[40]

4.7. Extremism, Fundamentalism, Liberalism, and Conservatism.

These tendencies have in various ways affected the progress of interfaith relationships in Nigeria. It is not enough for any religion to say, we have nothing to do with extremists, with fundamentalists; or, extremists do not speak for our respective religion. Indeed, extremists and fundamentalists do refer to the same sacred texts; they even, at times, portray themselves as the faithful interpreters and keepers of those sacred texts. Religious extremists can contribute to conflict escalation. They see radical measures as necessary to fulfilling God's wishes. Fundamentalists of any religion tend to take a Manichean view of the world. If the world is a struggle between good and evil, it is hard to justify compromising with the devil. Any sign of moderation can be decried as selling out, as abandoning God's will.

Next to extremism and fundamentalism are liberalism and conservatism. Liberals and conservatives of all the faiths are involved in different ways. Liberals are at home in dialogue, trialogue, and interfaith activities that are open to far ranging discussion about the issues of modern life and tend to believe their faiths need to respond to these by reinterpreting the meaning of fundamental principles in an evolving context. They will be happy to open up the dialogue table to a wider range of partners but they sometimes find it difficult to deal with firmly conservative positions, particularly on topics such as the role of women or same-sex relationships. Liberals also in most cases see themselves as superior to the conservatives by thinking and acting as people on the "right" path of progress with new ideas unlike the "old fashioned" conservatives.

---

[40] Dialogue and Proclamation, 52.

The conservative involvement in interfaith encounter is rather like that of participants in a stately dance where no one touches and everyone's space is respected. Conservatives will come together so that their religions can make common cause on particular issues or so that particularly burning issues can be discussed. The parameters for dialogue/trialogue are likely to reflect a more exclusivist notion of whether salvation or enlightenment can be found through a religious tradition other than one's own and a strong sense that one's own tradition and its practices are not likely to alter or change in response to encounters with other faiths. Such participants are particularly sensitive to the risk that inter faith encounters lead to syncretism or compromises their faith. Any interfaith initiative genuinely wanting to bring conservatives into the circle of trialogue within the faiths needs to reassure them that they will not have to compromise or water down their tradition.

In sum, any fruitful interfaith relationships should include an education and understanding of the dangers of extremism, fundamentalism, liberalism and conservatism.

4.8. Socio-political factors.

In Nigeria, the strong connection between ethnicity and religion and between politics and religion can be a major setback in interfaith relationships. People from warring tribes or disagreeing ethnic groups and political affiliations find it extremely difficult to converge on religious ground. They find it difficult to isolate religion from ethnicity and politics. Political association, racial and ethnic factors have often aggravated intolerance and caused a lack of reciprocity in interfaith relationships which can lead to frustration.

4.9. An attempt to create one religion.

Many people feel threatened by interfaith because they feel its agenda is to create one religion or at least to say that all religions are the same. This may indeed be the case for some, who see an ultimate harmony in such a unitary one religion in Nigeria, just as several historical traditions have, at one time or another, felt that the world would be blessed if everyone converted to that particular tradition.

The overwhelming majority of those involved in interfaith activity, however, recognizes the richness and blessing of religious diversity and hope to learn something more from interfaith relationships about the Divine Reality. It should be noted that neither dialogue nor trialogue in the spirit of interfaith relationships in aimed a creating one religion, instead they are meant to enrich each others understanding of ones own religion and the religions of the other with the aim of promoting mutual trust and love towards one another and building a peaceful society. Interfaith trialogue in Nigeria, rather than creating one religion, is meant to create one harmonious and peaceful Nigeria where all, irrespective of religious faith, can live in peace and enjoy the freedom of worshipping God according to his or her faith tradition.

4.10. Suspicion of an ulterior motive to proselytize.

It is important to mention here a subtle danger that threatens the practice of interfaith relationships. This is the suspicion, well founded or not, that participants in the interaction and encounter have ulterior motives of proselytism. Some people even criticize interfaith relationships as being a new method, even a skillful maneuver, to bring the partners over to the ideology or to the faith of the one who has taken the initiative. It must be repeated again that true interfaith relationships presuppose that the participants have no intention of changing the others' religions or even instilling doubts regarding the faith of the others. Such intentions would be a parody or a betrayal to authentic interfaith relationships.[41]

4.11. Materialism and indifferentism.

Materialism, religious indifference, and the multiplication of religious sects, which have become prevalent in the Nigerian society today are also factors that create confusion and raise new problems and obstacle to interfaith relationships. For instance, with more than 50,000 different Christian denominations, multiple Muslims sects,

---

[41]   Borrmans, *Guidelines for Dialogue between Christians and Muslims*, 42.

and numerous traditional forms of worship, which one does one relate with, and which one represents a widely accepted view of their religion. That is to say, is it the Catholic Church, the Anglican, the Presbyterian, the Pentecostals, or the Indigenous Nigerian Christian Churches that represent the essence of Christianity in Nigeria? There is the Christian Association of Nigeria (CAN) and the Supreme Council for Islamic Affairs (SCIA), and the Organization of African Traditional Religion (OTRA), yet not all Christians churches in Nigeria identify with CAN, and not all Muslim sects agree with nor identify with the ideals of the SCIA (for example the Boko Haram Islamic group that caused the deadly religious violence that spread across four states in July 2009).

CHAPTER FIVE

WHAT DOES THE FUTURE HOLD?

Religious violence, discriminations, intolerance, conflicts and riots threaten the stability and unity of Nigeria as a nation and destroy the brotherhood that we share as one. As expressed in a statement issued by the lecturers of Ahmadu Bello University, Zaria, cited by Jan Boer, among the West African nations Nigeria has witnessed unprecedented religious attacks against life, property and places of worship in most of the major cities and towns, as well as unprecedented campaigns of violent religious politics that are clearly aimed against the survival of our country and directly threaten her continued survival as a single entity.[42]

Interfaith relationships, on the other hand, restore the hope and confidence in the role of religion as an instrument of unity, peace, harmony, stability, justice and brotherhood; elements upon which the survival and future of Nigeria depend. This final chapter of our research examines how religious communities in the spirit of interfaith relationships in collaboration with the Nigerian government can advance peace relationships among the various religio-ethnic groups in Nigeria.

---

[42] Jan H. Boer, *Nigeria's Decade of Blood: 1980-2002.* (Ontario, Canada: Essence Publishing, 2003), 107-108.

5.1 INTERFAITH RELATIONSHIP AND THE FUTURE OF NIGERIA.

Religious presence in Nigeria is a formidable phenomenon; a phenomenon that has the potential of steering the wheel of the nation either to a healthy future or doom. From the look of things, the future does not seem to be bright. In the words of O. A. Olukunle,

> The future is not particularly bright for religious dispositions in this country, not because there are not enough copies of the Bible and the Koran and not because there are not enough religious leaders to preach but precisely because the grounds have been prepared to make religion a lame duck.[43]

Making religion a lame duck in Nigerian society refers to the present situation in Nigeria where religious leaders undermine religious principles for political reasons and material gains. Religion in Nigeria is no longer an agent of moral transformation; it has become an instrument in winning elections and gaining political appointments.

The future of Nigeria does not depend only upon the political class alone; the religious community has a part to play in this, given the indispensible place of religion in Nigeria. Hence, to secure a future for the nation, the government and the religious communities in a spirit of interfaith relationships must form mediating structures, which are "indispensible to the moral reconstruction of the public life."[44] In a society characterized by crises of meaning (religiously, politically, economically, socially, ethically, and culturally), the government alone cannot alleviate these crises nor can it provide all

---

[43]   O. A. Olunkunle, "The Impact of Religion on Nigeria Society: The Future Perspective" (Paper presented at the 25th annual Religious Conference, University of Ibadan, Ibadan, 17-20 September 1999), 2.

[44]   Simeon Illesanmi, *Religious Pluralism and the Nigerian State*. (Ohio: Ohio University Center for International Studies, 1997), 225

the meanings and fulfillments that Nigerians of all class are longing for. There are a number of ways that the religious communities can collaborate with government in averting the collapse of the nation occasioned by religious violence.

5.1.1. Government involvement in Interfaith Relationships:

The 1999 Constitution of the Federal Republic of Nigeria did not forbid the government in collaborating or involving itself with religion in advancing meaningful development for a stable future of the nation. What the constitution forbids is the government attaching itself and identifying itself with any particular religion as to give the impression that such has become a state a religion. Therefore, in pursuing its responsibilities, the government, without advancing the cause of any of the three religions in Nigeria, is to collaborate and engage with interfaith religious bodies, organizations and faith communities, who are able to help with the management of social change and with the promotion of cohesion. Faith-communities wish to influence government policies and are an important source of core values for societies. There is a need for well-structured consultation arrangements for this engagement, which needs to be a two-way process, respecting the different roles of governments and faith-communities. The agenda of this engagement should concern social issues rather than theological ones.

It is important for governments to encourage and support the process of interfaith relationships among faith communities. The task of taking forward interfaith trialogue essentially falls on the religious communities, but government can play a role in encouraging the initiation of the trialogue and relationships in an atmosphere of mutual respect. According to Kabir Garba, "Efforts at engendering harmonious living among Nigerians despite diversity of culture and religion may remain a mirage unless government articulate their role and the role of religion in promoting interfaith dialogue boldly."[45]

---

[45] Kabir Alabi Garba, "How interfaith dialogue promotes national growth," in *The Guardian Newspaper*. Friday, April 04, 2008.

5.1.2. Interfaith social service and government efforts.

Religion has both personal and social dimensions. In the depths of people's souls, religious faith is truly a personal matter, but because this faith necessarily has a social expression, it cannot be restricted to the field of private life. Therefore, religions can bring common values into play in public life. It is precisely for this reason that interfaith organizations and religious communities are to share the government's burden of providing social service to the society. It is important that, as with other similar organizations, faith communities become practical means, in conjunction with the government, for the realization of the much-needed social services and the fast disappearing moral values in the public lives of the Nigerian people.

Social services provided by religious groups within the context of interfaith relationships have several distinctive qualities. First is its "regularity." Aside from providing humanitarian aid for unexpected incidents such as natural disasters, religious groups also provide day-to-day care through their financial support for public welfare causes such as the disabled, AIDS sufferers, child drop-outs, widows and widowers, family relationships, psychological and drug counseling and environmental protection. Second is its "continuity." This sort of service has always been a mission of religious groups, and a component of their longstanding traditions. Third is its quality of "transcending:" the social services rendered by interreligious or interfaith groups transcend ethnic and national boundaries. The fourth distinctive quality of the social service offered by interfaith groups is its "trustworthiness." Because it is founded on religious faith, the entire process of delivering the services is guided by and carried out by religious believers, thereby increasing its degree of trustworthiness, and this trustworthiness is upheld by a track record of many years' giving.

This type of partnership and commitment between the government and interfaith bodies has already been achieved in developed nations: many interfaith organizations are effective in mobilizing the broader public for social service and participation, and are being commended for their initiatives and contributions. The public welfare programs initiated by interreligious groups cover a broad area, from poverty elimination, crime prevention and battling drug and alcohol abuse, to helping refugees, providing health and medical assistance, and developing culture and education. These acts of care and service bring tangible benefits to people of low income, low formal education, and extreme vulnerability. These social functions of interfaith organizations have met with society's approval, promoting the relevance of religion to public space, nation building and social life. Religious organizations have become as important a pillar of society as government and enterprise.

5.1.3. Conflict prevention and management.

The government should recognize and promote religious leaders of all faiths and their role in conflict prevention and management. Religious leaders and believers have an important contribution to make to the process of conflict prevention and resolution, not only in the specific terms of mediation, resolution, or prevention, but also according to the dictum of the golden rule: do unto others what you would like to have done unto you. This is the precondition of every encounter, of every type of trialogue and cooperation. In addition, it stems from recognizing and promoting the human dignity of every human being, independent from his or her religious affiliation.

Over the years interfaith groups have done significant work in improving the relationships of the participating faith communities towards one another, but this work has been only of limited success, partly because of lack of resources and government involvement and partly because many people are not very interested in their own religion let alone other peoples' religions. In all, interfaith groups and the government collectively have a major preventative task of helping to remove causes of conflict by identifying and addressing certain triggers of conflict in the relationships between Muslims, Christians and ATR before they degenerate into violence. They can also make a valuable contribution to peace building after conflicts and violence has occurred.

5.1.4. Joint peace and reconciliation council.

To secure a brighter future for Nigeria in the face of frequent religious violence, the government in conjunction with the religious communities should establish a peace and reconciliation council. One attempt to facilitate peace and reconciliation is the creation of a National Peace Council with branches at state and local levels, which brings together a small but diverse group of civil, religious and spiritual individuals who are known and respected. This idea is not new in Nigeria. It has been tried out, but with minimal achievement because of its structure. As noted by John Paden,

> The idea of a National Peace Council, with representatives from Christian and Muslim communities, has been established in Abuja by the Obasanjo administration. Yet, the extension of such councils is most critical at the state and local levels, where much of the violence transpires. A national council may send a symbolic message of conflict resolution, but it may be remote from the realities in the ground.[46]

There are two major factors that I believe are the realities on the ground that are lacking in the Obasanjo established peace council. First, as noticed in the above quotation, members or representatives of the council were drawn from two religions only – Islam and Christianity – excluding ATR, which is also an officially recognized religion in Nigeria. How can the council make meaningful contributions when one vital stakeholder is left out? Secondly, the presence of the council and its operation was limited to Abuja, the federal capital territory of Nigeria, without extension to the state, local and even rural areas that are the theatre of civil, ethnic and religious conflicts. Without peace at the local level, prosperity is illusory. Peace and stability is a precondition for economic development. It might be interesting to note that Abuja has never recorded any act of ethnic or religious violence. Hence, there can be no meaningful progress from such a commission unless it is all-embracing and encompasses the three tiers of government in Nigeria. The Peace Council should also have chapters in secondary

---

46 John N. Paden, *Faith and Politics in Nigeria.* (Washington, D.C.: United States Institute of Peace Press, 2008), 63.

schools and tertiary institutions all over Nigeria where, as rightly observed by Paden, interfaith peace committees serve as informal shock absorbers and mediators and stand ready to intercede in crisis situations.[47]

The mission of the Peace Council is to demonstrate that peace is possible, and that effective interreligious collaboration to make peace is possible.

In a society where religion too often is used to justify division, hatred, and violence – and very seldom used to relieve these problems – the Peace Councilors offer an alternative: the example of religious leaders and government working effectively together to relieve suffering and make the society whole. It must be emphasized that the authority of the Peace Council depends upon the moral authority of its members.

The Peace Council is committed to working together for the common needs of the whole community of life. The Council will build bridges through the message of non-violence, compassion, human rights, and universal responsibility, individual and collective. The heart of the Peace Council's work is a commitment by the Peace Councilors to help one another in the practical peace making that has made each Peace Councilor a leader in his or her community. There is no single formula for the programs. They vary depending on what is needed in each area.

5.1.5. Interfaith and the media.

The role of the media is indispensible in promoting a culture of peace in Nigeria. Media communication plays a vital role in the prevention or promotion of conflicts caused by different faiths. Most media houses in Nigeria are government owned. The government in collaboration with faith communities should constantly sponsor programs and adverts that show the evils of religious violence and its consequences for the present and future survival of Nigeria.

It is vital to emphasize the need for accurate communication in preventing conflicts caused by different cultural or religious

---

[47] Ibid.

backgrounds. Such communication requires the resolve of all parties involved to exchange timely, relevant, credible, inclusive and unbiased information. In reporting religious issues in Nigeria, the media should practice objectivity and nationalism by putting the interest of the nation at the heart of their reportage. The survival of our collectivity is more important that any sectional religious segment interest. Although religious freedom must be promoted, it is necessary for the government, through the National Communications Commission (NCC), to stop the airing and broadcasting of religious programs that incite people and hamper the much-needed peace for national growth and stability. Bearing in mind our shared responsibility in the prevention of conflicts, interfaith groups are to maximize the use of digital media in conjunction with traditional forms of media.

5.1.6. Interfaith Relationships and Government Policies.

Apart from the colonial government's inclination to Islam through the process of indirect rule in northern Nigeria,[48] other government policies and appointments since independence tend to favor and promote one religion over others. Political actors in Nigeria openly, and for political reasons, identify with one religion or another at the expense of our national unity. This has been a major source of concern and in most cases reasons for religious conflicts in Nigeria. Pointing out government inclinations towards one religion contrary to the constitution of Nigeria, Anthony Njoku writes:

---

[48] Nigeria was colonized by Britain until 1960. Before the amalgamation of the North and South in 1914, the colonial masters adopted a system of indirect rule in the North. That is to say, the actual powers still rested in the Emirs (the Muslim rulers) of the Northern kingdoms, while the colonial masters acted as supervisors. The colonial masters never had direct contact with the people; they were only getting across their messages and policies indirectly to the people through the Emirs, who were the direct rulers.

With the achievement of independence in 1960, Nigeria's constitution declared it a secular state; there was no state religion and no religion to be treated in a preferential manner and to be supported by the state apparatus. In practice, however, the religions of the incumbent national and regional rulers have generally received tacit state support.[49]

Political leaders promoted government policies that openly led to religious violence in Nigeria. Examples of such include the policies that favored the membership of Nigeria in the Organization of Islamic Countries (OIC) and the introduction of the Shariah system in almost all the northern states of Nigeria. As noted by Toyin Falola,

> Interreligious conflicts and religious violence of sociopolitical nature are much more complicated and threatening to Nigeria's survival . . . Such causes of conflict – like the Christian perception that the Islamic intelligentsia wants to control the state – may be difficult to resolve without further violence[50]

Given the present interplay between religion and politics in Nigeria, is there a way out of the collapse of Nigeria because of religious violence? Should we remove religion from the Nigerian political society? Nigerians will say no to this second question because there is almost a consensus among Nigerians that "Religion and politics are not mutually exclusive. As an integral aspect of

---

[49]   Anthony Chukwudi Njoku, "Economy, Politics, and the Theological Enterprise in Nigeria," in *Religion, History, and Politics in Nigeria: Essays in Honor of Ogbu U. Kalu.* Chima J. Korie & G. Ugo Nwokeji (eds). (New York: University Press of America, 2005),146

[50]   Toyin Falola, *Violence in Nigeria: The Crisis of Religious Politics and Secular Ideologies.* (New York: University of Rochester Press, 1998), 297

culture, religion impacts politics and is in turn influenced and shaped by it."[51] They equally affirm that, "The scope and nature of these influences could be either positive or detrimental to the corporate existence of a pluralistic society."[52]

The only way forward therefore is for the government, true to the constitution's requirement not to adopt any religion as the state religion, to develop and advance policies that promote interfaith relationships, collaboration and religious harmony. Whatever is given to one religion as a right or privilege should be extended to all three religions. Such rights and privileges include the allocation of land for the building of places of worship, government sponsorship of religious pilgrimages, and creation and appointment of commissions for the purpose of mediating conflicts. It is of utmost importance that the Nigerian governments deal on equal terms with different religions.

The words of Falola on the way forward if Nigeria is to survive a major breakup because of religious conflicts cannot be ignored by both the government and religious communities. According to Falola,

> Given the difficult nature of Nigeria's problems, especially the protracted nature of conflicts in a society divided by religion, if the crisis is not to lead to the collapse of the state or the eventual breakup of the country, the management of politics and the economy must change dramatically. As have been demonstrated, religious violence and aggression involve more than religious beliefs; they also include the interplay of political, economic, and ethnic forces. Therefore, any attempt to seek solutions to violence [in Nigeria] or

---

[51] Afe Adogame, "Politicization of Religion and Religionization of Politics in Nigeria," in *Religion, History, and Politics in Nigeria: Essays in Honor of Ogbu U. Kalu.* Chima J. Korie & G. Ugo Nwokeji (eds). (New York: University Press of America, 2005), 135.

[52] Ibid.

even to intellectualize it must move beyond the sermons on love and tolerance, the search for correct ethics and common ground among the different religions, or the rather simplistic manipulation of flags and anthems to construct a so-called civil religion as the project of the nation-state.[53]

Nevertheless, government policy is deficient in many ways when it comes to matters involving the interaction of the religious communities and the state. There must be a reassessment of the past policies that have failed the nation. They must rebuild the socio-political fabric and implement effective legislation that will put in place policies that ensure better state-interreligious relations. This entails that the religious communities and the government must be conscious of the fact that,

> Certain communicative and interactive conditions are unavoidable. Those in [political] power must know that they cannot destroy the beliefs and ideas of individuals and their groups. Nor must they create the impression that they favor one religion over another. To this extent, the constitutional provisions of religious freedom and the prohibition of the state from adopting any religion "as state religion" must be affirmed. The individual must also realize the citizenship of a greater Nigeria is more important than that of a partitioned country. Thus, a relationship of respect must be established between the state and its people. Various religious organizations also have to relate in such a way that their competition will not negate the primary objectives of the state that unites them . . . The individual and the state must recognize that the creation of a stable political community involves the acceptance and use of a variety of divergent ideas drawn from all ethnic groups and religions. Any one belief or insight drawn from a specific religion or group may cause

---

[53] Falola, *Violence in Nigeria*, 298.

suspicion . . . A long standing policy of divisiveness, based on the conviction that an idea, belief, or religion has to be vanquished so that a dominant one can create a hegemony, must be abandoned precisely because it has not worked and it has generated problems. If elements of any religion are found useful, they must be carefully presented so as not to alter any existing equilibrium or be legislated by coercion.[54]

5.2. RECOMMENDATIONS.

Interfaith relationships are not optional for the Nigerian religious communities and the nation as whole, as can be seen in this research; they are a necessity. Although the reality of religious violence and intolerance threatens the togetherness we share as one and the corporate survival of the Nigerian nation, not all hopes are lost. The religious communities and the government in the spirit of interfaith relationships have a commitment to strengthen the peace and harmony of the nation and to avoid all that can lead to violence and conflict in the name of religion. To achieve this, I recommend the following.

5.2.1. To the Government.

To foster peace and unity in a diverse religious society like Nigeria the government should consider the following:

5.2.1.1. Security.

We cannot talk about peace in the absence of security. Much loss of life and property during religious violence in Nigeria has been blamed on the lack of adequate security. As observed by Human Rights Watch,

> The federal government and security forces bear a heavy responsibility for the massive loss of life in Yelwa and Kano. In Yelwa, the security forces were absent during the attack of May 2-3. Around 700 people had already

---

[54] Ibid, 302.

been killed by the time the army intervened. Likewise in Kano, around 200 people had been killed before peace was restored. Then, instead of protecting those at risk and trying to arrest the perpetrators, some of the police and soldiers deployed to Kano carried out dozens of extrajudicial killings, contributing further to the violence. Their actions in Kano were typical of the response of the security forces to previous outbreaks of inter-communal violence in other parts of Nigeria.[55]

The key recommendation to the government is for the timely deployment of an adequate security force presence in areas of likely tension and improved mechanisms to obtain reinforcements rapidly should the need arise, while at the same time ensuring that members of the security forces do not carry out extrajudicial killings.

Efforts should be made to anticipate and prevent violence, rather than just reacting after violence has already begun. These efforts include beefing up security in all parts of the country and not tolerating proliferation of arms in any form; pursuing programs of disarmament and initiatives to encourage people to hand in weapons, and strengthening controls over weapons flow and improving border security with neighboring countries. Hints of breach of the peace should not be allowed to get out of hand before they are nipped in the bud. I strongly agree with NIREC's conviction "that prior and timely evaluation of early warning signals or intelligence reports by state security agencies is a necessary step in averting the doom of religious violence in Nigeria."[56]

Furthermore, the government should give strict instructions to members of the Nigerian police and military deployed who quell rioting that force should never be used against individuals who are unarmed and are not taking part in violence or other criminal

---

[55]   Human Rights Watch. *Revenge in the Name of Religion: The Cycle of Violence in Plateau and Kano States.* May 25, 2005. p. 4. http://www.hrw.org (assessed: October 1, 2009)

[56]   Abbas Jimoh, "Jos Crisis: NIREC demands judicial inquiry," in *Daily Trust.* Thursday December 4, 2008.

activities. In addition, members of the security forces should make every effort to arrest individuals suspected of criminal activity without resorting to lethal force. All members of the security forces should respect the U.N. Code of Conduct for Law Enforcement Officials and the U.N. Basic Principles on the Use of Force and Firearms by Law Enforcement officials. Their conduct should also be monitored to ensure that these standards are adhered to at all times.

5.2.1.2. Arrest and prosecution of culprits.

In addition to ensuring adequate security, members of the security forces should make every effort to arrest individuals suspected of criminal activity without resorting to lethal force. However, it is one thing to arrest and another thing to prosecute those arrested. In Nigeria, those arrested are most often set free without any charges pressed against them. None prosecution of perpetrator and planners of religious violence has multiplied in frequency. As expressed by NIREC at the occurrence of the 2008 Jos Crisis,

> One of the causative factors is that past happenings have not been punished and we feel for this issue to be put at permanent rest, anybody found to have been involved in this crisis (*sic*) , be it a Muslim or Christian should be punished. This is one of the points we are going to emphasize in the course of the hearings of the judicial commission of inquiry, if it is set up.[57]

Hence, the government should make justice a priority by ensuring that individuals responsible for organizing and carrying out religious violence in the country are identified, arrested, charged, and tried promptly, including members of the security forces, according to international fair trial standards.

5.2.1.3. Interfaith and peace initiatives.

---

[57] Ibid.

The government should encourage trialogue and conflict resolution between ethnic and religious communities in Nigeria, at the grassroots as well as leadership levels. Conflict resolution initiatives should not preclude the search for justice, which should ensure that all Nigerians are able to enjoy the same rights, regardless of their place of origin or residence, and address issues at the heart of disputes between communities, such as control of local political positions, economic resources and ownership of land.

5.2.1.4. Addressing poverty and unemployment.

One of the major causes of violence apart, from doctrinal differences, is poverty and unemployment. A hungry and unemployed person will take anything within his reach to make a living, including hiring himself as an instrument of violence in the hands of some politicians and fanatical religious people. This has been part of the problem in Nigeria. For example in the 1980 riots, most of the participants were poor and unemployed, and religion was used to express the protest. Other riots reflected the concern of the poor for the economic mismanagement of the country, the widening gap between the rich and poor, and the wide-ranging deprivations.[58]

To tackle the problem of religious violence honestly, the government – federal, state and local – has to work to address the issues of poverty through job creation and vocational training for young people. The gap between the rich and poor has to be bridged or at least reduced considerably, and the inequality between ethnic groups and areas has to be addressed. The government has to initiate a people-oriented development strategy that will empower all citizens, allow them to lead creative and useful lives, and enable them to pursue their beliefs within the confines of established regulations and a stable political system.

5.2.1.5. Publish and Implement findings and recommendations of commissions of inquiry.

---

[58]   Falola, *Violence in Nigeria*, 298.

The government's usual response to outbreaks of violence in Nigeria, over the last few years, has been to set up commissions of inquiry. Many such commissions have been set up to determine the immediate and remote causes of religious conflicts and violence in different parts of the country, but regrettably Nigerians are constantly kept in the dark as to the findings and implementations of recommendations from such commissions. Only a few of such commissions have published their reports, and even when they have, their recommendations have rarely been acted upon or have led to prosecutions. In relation to events in Plateau State, the federal and state governments have set up several such commissions of inquiry since the September 2001 violence in Jos. A judicial commission of inquiry set up by the Plateau state government, chaired by Judge Niki Tobi, held public hearings and received numerous submissions on the 2001 Jos crisis. Its report was never published, although it was reported to have been one of many documents submitted to the peace conference, which took place under the state of emergency in 2004. A judicial commission of inquiry was also set up on "civil disturbances in Shendam, Langtang North, Langtang South and Wase local government areas"⁵⁹ and produced a report in June 2003, which has not been published either. A judicial commission of inquiry at the federal level, with a broader remit to investigate the conflicts in Plateau and three other Middle Belt states (Nasarawa, Benue and Taraba), was set up in 2002. It concluded its hearings and submitted its report to the presidency in April 2003; by early 2005, its report had still not been published and its conclusions were not known.⁶⁰ Even until today, there is no evidence that the report has been published.

To show its seriousness in handling, preventing, reducing and ending religious conflicts in Nigeria, the government must in the spirit of justice and accountability, publish the findings of previous

---

⁵⁹ Ezekiel Karunga, "The plateau Unity and Reconciliation Bill," *This Day*, October 13, 2004.

⁶⁰ Human Rights Watch. *Revenge in the Name of Religion*, 36-37.

and subsequent commissions of inquiries while diligently acting upon recommendations made by such commissions.

5.2.1.6. Defining the institutional roles in religious tolerance and interfaith relationships.

Largely, institutions (government/state and religious) are essential to the maintenance of peace and order within Nigerian society. The institutions in Nigeria have not always been employed in the right direction towards ensuring mutual co-existence and lasting peace among people of different religions in the spirit of interfaith relationships. To re-write this wrong, I am advocating the following institutional roles in advancing the cause of religious peace and tolerance in Nigeria.

a.) Nigeria should create a Ministry of Religious Affairs or at least a Secretariat for Interfaith Relations under the ministry of Internal Affairs. This ministry, headed by an expert in the history of religion in Nigeria and interfaith activities, will oversee religious issues involving all the religions in the country and coordinate among bodies promoting dialogue, trialogue and interfaith activities in Nigeria. This ministry will function to disseminate the culture of tolerance and understanding through the use of media, national orientations, conferences and symposia, as well as developing relevant cultural, educational and media programs. This ministry will work in urging government and religious bodies to issue documents that stipulate respect for religions and their symbols, the prohibition of the denigration of religious symbols and the repudiation of those who commit such acts. It will develop rules to be approved by the National Assembly on how to apportion credit or blame to religious bodies in times of peace and crisis, just as it has created the ministry on Niger Delta to address the issue of development and militancy in the Niger Delta and South-South Geopolitical Zone.

b.) Every university, tertiary institution, and secondary school in Nigeria should pay particular attention to the study of religion. Not just religion, but comparative religion or history or philosophy of religion depending on what name a particular school may want to call it. It should no longer be the present system of Christians studying only Christian religious knowledge and its teaching only in the so-called "Christian" states or zones; and Muslims studying only Islamic religious knowledge and its teaching only in the so-called "Islamic" states or zones. Presently, the teaching of Christian Religious Knowledge is banned in public schools (at the elementary and secondary levels) in the Northern/ Islamic states and the same applies to the teaching of Islam in some of the southern zones, especially the south-east zone. This exclusive approach leaves students completely ignorant or uninformed about the religions of others. Moreover, African Traditional Religion is not a subject of study in any elementary or high school in Nigeria. Our religious curriculum is still that which we inherited from or which was influenced by the colonial missionaries that presented native and traditional religion as evil and sinful, and followers of it as pagans and heathens. If we wish to make any real headway toward achieving lasting peace among the religions in Nigeria, I recommend that all three religions be included in the curriculum of both elementary and high schools in Nigeria and their study made compulsory for all.

c.) Developed nations strive in research in all disciplines including religion. I am therefore making a case for the establishment of a national institute for the research and study of religion in the six geopolitical zones in Nigeria. This is a novel idea, but it will develop a better understanding of the religious landscape of Nigeria in general and in the zones in particular. This institute will conduct research on the immediate and remote causes of violence and conflict in Nigeria and the zones, and develop a possible blueprint for peaceful and mutual coexistence. It will have a working team of experts to study the problems hindering and preventing trialogue and interfaith relationships. It will also prepare a study that provides vision for the solution of these problems. This institute will help people to learn about the religion of the other not for scholarly purposes but for pragmatic purposes.

Currently *ad hoc* committees are set up as a response to violence or conflict. For example after the Kaduna religious – Sharia crisis of 2000, the presidential address to the nation by President Olusegun Obasanjo revealed how the issue of religious violence is handled in Nigeria. In his words, as cited by Oranika:

> It was clear to me that while a toll was being taken of the massive losses that attended the disturbances, it was necessary to immediately begin the process of healing and reconciliation. I met leaders of the factions and groups involved – the religious and political leaders. We explored all possible ways of bringing the carnage to a permanent halt and reached agreement on a number of issues.[61]

Such ad-hoc committees in the midst of ill feelings over loss of life and property cannot come up with reasonable, well-articulated, rational and lasting solutions. This is an emergency solution to a problem that is becoming almost perennial. At times, the committee

---

[61] Paul Oranika, *Nigeria: One Nation, Two Systems.* (Baltimore: PublishAmerica, 2004), 42.

is given a two-week or two-month deadline to perform a herculean task. It is doubtful that it can bear any lasting fruit given the present religious circumstances in Nigeria. The national institute, I am recommending, will constantly, rigorously, and objectively look back into the distant past and the present and apply its findings forward to a distant future. It will have time to learn from and exchange ideas with other nations with multi-religious populations in order to examine how they are living together without violence, and, in violent situations, how they are able to reach a resolution within a short period without the terrible loss of life and property as is the case in Nigeria.

5.2.2. To the Religious Community.

Like the government, the faith communities and religious bodies in Nigeria, both as one in the spirit of interfaith relationships and as individual religious group, have an obligation towards ensuring the peace and stability of Nigeria and advancing the role of religion in the formation of character and moral rectitude. To achieve this, I recommend the following.

5.2.2.1. From institutional approach to interpersonal approach.

For years and decades, interfaith relationships in Nigeria have been institutionalized. The emphasis has been on the Christian Association of Nigeria (CAN) and the Supreme Council of Islamic Affairs in Nigeria. It has centered on "leading Imams, Christian leaders and traditional rulers,"[62] and has gone from one committee of scholars, political and religious leaders to another. This can be seen in Jan Boer's report on the Kaduna crisis:

> The Kaduna State Government relaxed the curfew from 24 hours to 12, and inaugurated a 5-man judicial commission to investigate this week's two days of rioting by Christian and Muslim youths . . . The commission which has four weeks to conclude its assignment is under the chairmanship of Justice Ja'afaru Dalhat. Other

---

[62] Oranika, *One Nation, Two Systems*, 46.

members are Alhaji Akilu Idris, Mr. P. Y. Lolo, Mr.
Victor Gwani and Alhaji Tukur Usman. Mr. Dominic
G. Yahaya would serve as secretary, while Mr. Gamaliel
Kure is the commission's counsel.[63]

As we can see, these measures towards lasting peace and mutual
coexistence among the religions are only institutional approaches.
Most of the time, those involved in these institutions are rarely a
part of the conflict nor are they ever present at the scene of the
violence. Those who are the actual participants, culprits and victims
are left out of these institutional approaches. Again, even when a
committee approach is necessary, appointments to such committees
are politicized. Those who are appointed may be experts in their
various fields of endeavor but have little knowledge of matters of
religion and interfaith activities. This is evident from the constitution
of the commission cited above. The members were experts and
accomplished scholars in the fields of law, economics, military, and
politics, but were not experts in religious matters.

Having carefully observed the ineffectiveness of the institutional
approach to religious violence and interfaith relationships among the
religions in Nigeria, I am recommending a change of emphasis and
approach: From an institutional approach to an interpersonal and
daily life approach, from an academic or committee, approach to a
communion and faith sharing approach. In this new approach, true
reconciliation, healing, tolerance, and other interfaith activities will
begin with the actual victims of religious violence and intolerance.
This approach entails a live religious partner, a real person you can
keep in touch with, walk along with in the same community and
environment, understand and see each other as brothers, sisters,
and friends, and not first of all as members of different religious
affiliations. It entails emptying of one's cup (being open to learn
and to remove one's biases and prejudices against the other). It
entails sharing table and meal fellowship while being conscious

---

[63] Jan H. Boer, *Nigeria's Decade of Blood, 1980-2002.* (Ontario
Canada: Essence Publishing, 2003), 120,128.

of the other's dietary laws, and sharing worship fellowship. I unconsciously, without having any interfaith activity in mind, but in living my daily life, practiced what I am proposing in one of the parishes where I served. It was a powerful means of witnessing and promoting peace, love, unity to each other, without spoken words on religious dogmas and doctrines. In this approach, people realize more consciously, who they are: a people living together with each other, and committed to the common good of all. This I believe is far more effective than the institutional approach. Note that I am not condemning institutional contributions in religious tolerance and interfaith relationships. Institutions are important, but not in the way that they have been used in Nigeria

5.2.2.2. Going back to the roots of our tradition before Islam and Christianity came to Nigeria: Can anything be learned?

One question that comes to mind is this: prior to the coming of foreign religions – Christianity and Islam—to Nigeria, how did Nigerians with more than 250 ethnic groups, having different languages, cultures, and modes of practicing traditional religions, and can we learn anything from the past so that we can better address the present day religious situation in Nigeria?

The current trend in the public practice of religion in Nigeria in general and in the South-East in particular has been to ignore the traditional roots of the people. Traditional religion has been presented either as a dying religion or as an obsolete and evil religion with nothing to offer in this 21st century. Nevertheless, this is a questionable approach to the understanding and practice of religion.

Hence, in this work, I am recommending a return to our traditional ATR values or at least a re-examination of these traditional values by followers of Islam and Christianity. For example, what are the values that helped the people to live together as one, their different modes of life and worship not withstanding, before the advent of Christianity and Islam in Nigeria and Igbo land in particular? What did these two foreign religions bring to the zone that ushered in conflict, intolerance, and violence in an area that hitherto had a peaceful religious atmosphere? There were tribal wars occasioned by land disputes, but not religious wars, even though various tribes had their own forms of traditional religion before the advent of Islam and Christianity. What can we learn from our traditional roots and values that will facilitate and promote interfaith relationships in this zone?

Honest answers to these questions will definitely enhance and improve relationships among followers of different religions living together within the same community. As observed by Friday Mbon,

> Indeed, many contemporary Nigerians [irrespective of religious affiliations] are now beginning to be aware of the need to return to the traditional socio-religious ethics of their fore parents. That is what many of them recently strongly recommended to the Political Bureau, a body responsible for working out the best political structure for Nigeria's next republic. That, too, was the recommendation of the President Shagari's Committee on Ethical Re-orientation in 1982 – a recommendation to go back to the African traditional ethical system in which the welfare of individual was a function and consequence of the welfare of the community; an ethical system in which the individual was happy only if and when the community was happy. The essence of this kind of ethical system was the preservation and integration of social as well as spiritual life. The background of this ethical system [informed by the religious background] was traditional African societies' concern for each other; its goal was to unite members of the community into one great harmonious family in which each one continued to seek the good and welfare of the many.[64]

---

[64] Friday M. Mbon, "African Traditional Socio-Religious Ethics and National Development: The Nigerian Case," in *African Traditional Religions in Contemporary Society*, Jacob K. Olupona (eds). (New York: Paragon House, 1991), 107.

Many things can be learned from ATR that will enhance the spirit of togetherness among the religious communities in Nigeria.

5.2.2.3. A commitment to peace and interfaith by religious leaders.

Nigerians generally look more to their leaders rather than to systems for examples in religious and civil life. Aware of this fact, religious leaders should:

a.) Refrain from making statements that incite violence or encourage hostility and prejudice towards other ethnic or religious communities. In situations of potential tension, they are to, explicitly and publicly, call on members of their community to refrain from resorting to violence, and make clear that retaliatory attacks in the name of self-defense are never a justification for killing or other forms of violence against unarmed civilians. They should continue to seek long-term solutions to the tensions and grievances among communities and pursue meaningful dialogue/trialogue about peaceful ways of resolving these tensions at all levels.

b.) They should constantly organize inter-religious and inter-cultural meetings, seminars and activities that will promote better relationships among the followers of different religions with a view of advancing the culture of peace, understanding and coexistence.

c.) All religious leaders concerned about the increasingly militant profile of their faith, even those who occupy a relatively humble position, should take the initiative in reclaiming the compassionate core of their own tradition. They should re-examine the teachings and or texts in their own traditions that have incited their co-religionists to aggression and hatred, examining the context in which these teachings and or texts were created and seeing how

they relate to the tradition as a whole; and engage
in a creative critique of teaching and preaching
methods. Before castigating other traditions, they
should study the history of their own failings. Such
self-criticism is imperative and central in all the
three religions in Nigeria.

d.) Religious leaders are to remain mindful that their
religions must not identify themselves with political,
economic, or social powers, so as to remain free to
work for justice and peace. They should not forget
that confessional political regimes might do serious
harm to religious values as well as to society.

5.2.2.4. A commitment to peace, harmony and interfaith by
followers of various religious traditions.

Besides the role of religious leadership in ensuring peace and
harmony as well as encouraging interfaith relationships among the
three religions in Nigeria, the lay faithful have an equal responsibility
to live out their religious call of interaction and fellowship with
the followers of other religions. To achieve this, I recommend the
following:

a.) Followers of all religions should reach across sectarian
divides to recover a strong appreciation of their
common values and call to love and brotherhood.

b.) In the same spirit of justice and respect, religious
groups should discourage double standards and the
demonization of others. They should desist from
name-calling and the watering down of the teaching
and doctrines of other faiths. Name calling and
mud-slinging in any form is harmful to the cause of
peace and reconciliation

c.) There should be a serious examination of the
ideology and mythology of "fundamentalist" or
extremist religious groups. They should not be
simply dismissed as the lunatic fringe, ignored,
or regarded with secularist disdain, because their

teachings often express fears and anxieties that no society can safely ignore.

d.) Followers of religions are to be encouraged to be open and to learn about other religious traditions. This can be acquired through formal education, enlightenment speeches, and above all by daily interactions (e.g. attending and observing religious gatherings and activities of others). Open-minded questions that seek enriching information about the religion of others should be encouraged. This sort of openness and willingness to learn may prove to be an efficient means of combating fanaticism, prejudices and stereotypes.

e.) More thought needs to be given to why the present interfaith activities in Nigeria most often exclude ATR and how this might be changed. It is a vital point, as we need to be very aware of the dangers of exclusivist tendencies in religious matters.

It is strongly recommended that both government and religious communities implement these recommendations for enhancing interfaith relationships among followers of religion in Nigeria.

CHAPTER SIX

FINAL EVALUATION AND CONCLUSION.

This series of interfaith in Nigeria has been presented in three volumes, with a core emphasis on examining the place and role of religion in Nigeria from a trialogical interfaith perspective. It has ascertained that Nigeria is a pluralistic society with multi-religious traditions majorly divided along African Traditional Religion (ATR), Islam and Christianity.

Relationships among these religions have some times been friendly, cooperative and interactive either as one religion to another or as three of them coming together in the spirit of interfaith relationships. However, most times, such relationships have been characterized by discriminations, intolerance, violence, conflicts and riots leading to the loss of property and thousands of lives. These conflicts are not limited to any particular religion; religious violence and conflicts have occurred between the three religions: Christians and Muslims; Muslims and ATR; Christians and ATR; Muslims and Muslims; and ATR, Muslims, and Christians simultaneously. It has also occurred along the lines of ethnic and political divides. Muslims have also fought against the government, causing ATR and Christian casualties. Generally, the northern states have been the center and the origin of most violence involving Muslims and Christians, Muslims and Muslims, and religio-ethnic conflicts. The south, while witnessing few conflicts involving Christians and Muslims, has been the center and origin of conflicts involving Christianity and ATR.

Despite doctrinal and other socio-political causes of religious violence in Nigeria, this work reveals that religious violence is also frequently an expression of frustration with inequalities or perceived marginalization, mostly from the government whose policies tend to favor a particular religion at the expense of peace and public harmony. Under extreme poverty and hard economic conditions, religious violence becomes an avenue for grievances against and challenges to the current politics of resource distribution. The riots of the late 1980's and 1990's could be explained as having links with the circumstances described above.

There is no one way by which religious violence has occurred in Nigeria. Some have been spontaneous, some premeditated, and some revenge missions. The extent and degree of damage depends largely on the nature of conflicts and who are involved. For example, religious violence that bears on doctrine and ethnicity is often nationwide and causes more casualties. Such were the Shariah riots of 2000 that began between Muslims, Christians, and traditionalists in the northern city of Kaduna and spread to neighboring towns and eastern cities

The wounds of division and pains of religious conflicts have been far reaching, leaving children orphaned, many families rendered homeless, business owners turned jobless overnight, and many widowed. The material and financial costs have been enormous for the nation as a whole. The future seems to be bleak, with no hope of rebuilding and interacting. In this midst of dark clouds, this work sees hope and better future for Nigeria and the religious communities. Where lays this hope? It is in interfaith relationships with a strong and firm commitment on the part of the government and the religious communities.

Interfaith activity has been identified in this work as a major component in and contributor towards promoting peace and co-existence between people and communities of faith. People from a wide variety of countries and conflicts have used interfaith dialogue/trialogue and action as a medium for more harmonious co-existence. During the preparatory stage of this work, I came across many examples that show that interfaith relationships can help heal wounds and feelings of injustice, isolation, and inequality. A good example of this is the case of the Imam and the Pastor. As people of different faiths meet and get to know each other better, they will begin to talk about a range of issues. Some will discuss theology and philosophy; others will want to learn about ways of prayer and meditation. Some will want to engage together in social action or witness. Some government officials and agencies are also becoming more aware of the important contribution that faith communities can make to national life.

Interfaith relationships have a lot to contribute to Nigeria's diverse religious and ethnic society. Nevertheless, they also have weaknesses, especially when certain principles and guidelines as explained in this book are not followed. Among the strengths is that interfaith relationships can help:

◊ To eliminate ignorance and reduce stereotyping and prejudice about particular religions and religious communities;

◊ To lay firm foundations to overcome differences or to meet common goals at local and national levels by building confidence and trust through rational dialogue/trialogue and co-operative actions;

◊ To link relevant religious and multinational organizations to reduce violent responses to situations by improving communication, facilitating; dialogue/trialogue and deep listening, addressing perceived injustices, and understanding and respecting different value systems;

◊ Promote dialogue/trialogue and harmony between and within religions and help people recognize, and respect other religions' search for truth and wisdom.

The very existence of interfaith activities is strength. If we do things together, whatever they are, we both show others that collaboration is possible and get to know other faith traditions better through the people we work with. Interfaith work has not just stayed at the level of top leaders. Works done at the grassroots level are all useful ways of incorporating more people into understanding better what other faith traditions are about. The different interfaith organizations span a wide range of activities: education, youth, spiritual sharing, development, peace reconciliation, and inter-cultural activities. Interfaith organizations may be able to provide a neutral venue where those on opposite sides can meet. Members of different faiths can join in prayers for peace, as they have done on many occasions in different parts of the country

Besides the strengths of interfaith relationships in peace processes and harmonious co-existence, there are some weaknesses associated with such relationships. These include:

◊ The risk of interfaith dialogue/trialogue lapsing into "clubby circles" in which bonds of friendship among the privileged few who can attend national and regional conferences may be formed but without any specific focus. This could result in the relationships failing to turn into transformative action in our societies and thus, implicitly, supporting the status quo.

◊ The danger that interfaith worship tends to be artificial.

◊ That possibility that interfaith work is carried out solely by the "progressive" sectors/people of the different religions, leaving out the majority who either are indifferent to other faiths or think that they are nowhere near God or the Truth.

◊ The danger of a shallow spirituality in interfaith activities. We need to ground interfaith work deeper in the spirituality of the different faith traditions involved. There have been fears expressed that the interfaith movement is hardly to be distinguished in character from the secular NPO/NGO'S. The need to find better ways of worshipping together is part of this point.

However, it must be pointed out that the strengths of interfaith relationships out-weigh their weaknesses.

I would like to re-emphasize that if the guidelines for fruitful interfaith are followed, commitments made and the activities implemented, then interfaith relationships in Nigeria will yield the following blessings:

◊ Those engaged in trialogue will gain a greater knowledge of each other's religious tradition. Through this, they can overcome their respective prejudices, misunderstandings and negative stereotypes. Hence mutual understanding can develop.

◊ Participants will be in a position to see the good present in other religions.

◊ We may integrate into our own lives the spiritual riches and values of other religions, thus enriching our religious insights and values.

◊ It opens us to the deficiencies and failures of our own religious traditions and we can make resolutions to correct them.

◊ If we are in dialogue with other religions, especially those we live with in the same vicinity, we can better respond to natural and human calamities in order to create a world of harmony, peace and love.

◊ The corrected deficiencies and failures in our own religious traditions, motivated by values from other religions, will enable us to acknowledge God's work in us and in others. Thus working for peace, justice and love will become easier.

In conclusion, it will be good to remember that in the eyes of many, religion is inherently conflictual and a source of violence rather than an instrument of peace it portends to be. To correct this impression, one should promote a heightened awareness of the positive peace building and reconciliatory role religion has played in many conflict situations within and outside Nigeria. More generally, fighting ignorance can go a long way. Where silence and misunderstanding are all too common, learning about other religions would be a powerful step forward. Being educated about other religions does not mean conversion but may facilitate understanding and respect for other faiths. Communicating in a spirit of humility and engaging in self-criticism would also be helpful.

Again, to ensure a stable society devoid of conflicts, religious and otherwise, Nigerians must let go of favoritism, nepotism, oppression, marginalization, and ensure that justice is done to all sections. Followers of African Traditional Religion, Muslims and Christians would do well to observe, practice and uphold the principles of their religions that call for love, tolerance, unity, compassion, justice, non-violence and peace, in a spirit of dialogue, trialogue and interfaith relationships.

While this series on interfaith relationships claims to be in-depth and thorough and, without ambiguity, the most elaborate and comprehensive in the field of Nigeria's interfaith relationships – with a novel emphasis on trialogical relationships – it does not claim to have the final word in this field. Having been built on the foundation of other scholars in the religious climate of Nigeria and South-east geopolitical zone, it is hoped that it will contribute to further research by scholars of religious studies within and outside Nigeria. It may also elicit ideas on how to advance peace and harmony and avert religious conflict in Nigeria and other countries polarized by religious violence and conflict.

May we end this work with a firm commitment on behalf of the three religions in Nigeria:

We are "stewards of our community of faith" coming from multi-ethnic/religious traditions. As stewards, we receive God's gifts of creation, brotherhood, peace and diversity gratefully, cultivate them responsibly and share them lovingly in justice. With deep faith and trust in God and in one another, conscious of togetherness as one and not forgetting our diversity, we move forward to building a better Nigeria. As we make this commitment, may we always remember that this is:

◊ *The time to acknowledge and celebrate that things need not be what they have been, that the future need not repeat the ugly past.*

◊ *The time for sorting out what of the past must be forgiven and set aside, and what of the past is worthy to be grasped and handed on, built upon, made our own and given to future generations.*

◊ *The time when we as Nigerians must pause, repent and give thanks for all that we have, and look forward to a better Nigeria where all can worship freely according to the dictates of a good conscience guided by the noble truths of ones' religions without violence, discrimination and conflict; and see in the faces of all Nigerians, irrespective of religion and ethnicity, a brother, a sister and a friend.[65]*

Together as one, we will favor peace, harmony and fellowship that binds us together as a people of faith living in one nation. Through interfaith activities, we will counter the tendencies of religious individuals and communities who promote cultures of intolerance, violence and conflict in society. We recognize and praise the non-violent peacemakers. We disown violence and killing in the name of religion.

---

[65] This statement is adapted from the United State Conference of Catholic Bishops' statement of the Jubilee Year 2000. http://www. usccb.org/

BIBLIOGRAPHY

1. Achebe, Chinua. *Things Fall Apart*. New York: Anchor Books, 1994.
2. Adogame, Afe. "Politicization of Religion and Religionization of Politics in Nigeria", in *Religion, History, and Politics in Nigeria: Essays in Honor of Ogbu U. Kalu*. Edited by Chima J. Korieh & Ugo G. Nwokeji. New York: University of America Press, 2005.
3. Baum, Gregory. "The Socio Context of American Catholic Theology," in *Catholic Theology in North American Context: Current Issues in Theology (CTSA Proceedings)*. George Kilkourse (ed.). Macon: Mercer University Press, 1986.
4. Baum, Gregory. "Religious pluralism and Common Values." *The Journal of Religious Pluralism*. 4.1988.
5. Blears, Hazel. ed. *Faces to Face and Side by Side: A framework for partnership in our multi-faith Society*. London: Communities and Local Government Publication, 2008.
6. Boer, Jan H. *Nigeria's Decade of Blood, 1980-2002*. Ontario Canada: Essence Publishing, 2003.
7. Borrmans, Maurice. ed., *Interreligious Document, Vol. I: Guidelines for Dialogue between Christians*

and Muslims (Pontifical Council for Interreligious Dialogue.) New York: Paulist Press, 1990.

8. Boss, Marc. "Religious Diversity: From Tillich to Lindbeck and Back." In *Religion in the New Millennium: Theology in the Spirit of Paul Tillich.* Raymond F. Bulman & Frederick J. Parrella, Eds. Macon, Georgia: Mercer University Press, 2001.

9. Dialogue. *Dictionary.com Unabridged* (v 1.1). Radom House, Inc. http://dictionary.reference.com/browse/dialog.

10. "dialogue" *Merriam-Webster Online Dictionary.* 2008. http://www.merriam-webster.com/dictionary/dialogue

11. Dictionary: *TrialogueAnswers.com.* http://www.answers.com/trialogue

12. Ebije, Ayegba Israel. "Nirec Moves to Stop Religious Crisis in the Country." *Daily Trust.* January 23, 2009.

13. Falola, Toyin. *Violence in Nigeria: The Crisis of Religious Politics and Secular Ideologies.* New York: University of Rochester press, 1998.

14. Fārūqī, Ismāil Rājī al. *Trialogue of the Abrahamic Faiths.* Maryland: amana publications, 1995.

15. Garba, Kabir Alabi. "How interfaith dialogue promotes national growth," in *The Guardian Newspaper.* Friday, April 04, 2008.

16. Human Rights Watch. Revenge in the Name of Religion: The Cycle of Violence in Plateau and Kano States. May 25, 2005. http://www.hrw.org

17. Hussain, Amir. *Oil and Water: Two Faiths, One God.* (Ontario, Canada: CopperHouse, 2006.

18. Ilesanmi, Simeon O. *Religious Plurality and the Nigerian State.* Ohio: Center for

International Studies, 1997.

19. Jimoh, Abbas. "Jos Crisis: NIREC demands judicial inquiry," in *Daily Trust.*
Thursday December 4, 2008.

20. Karunga, Ezekiel. "The plateau Unity and Reconciliation Bill," *This Day.* October 13, 2004.

21. Kessler, Gary E. *Philosophy of Religion: Toward a Global Perspective.* Belmont, CA: Wadsworth Publishing Company, 1999.

22. Knitter, Paul F. *One Earth Many Religion: Multifaith Dialogue and Global responsibility.* Maryknoll, NY Orbis Books, 1995.

23. Korieh, Chima J. & Ugo G. Nwokeji. *Religion, History, and Politics in Nigeria: Essays in Honor of Ogbu U. Kalu.* New York: University Press of America, Inc., 2005.

24. Mbon, Friday M. "African Traditional Socio-Religious Ethics and National Development: The Nigeria Case" in *African Traditional Religions in Contemporary Society,* edited by Jacob K. Olupona. New York: Paragon House, 1991.

25. McFedries, Paul. *Word Spy – Trialogue.* http://www.wordspy.com/words/trialogue.asp.

26. Njoku, Anthony Chukwudi. "Economy, Politics, and the Theological Enterprise in Nigeria," in *Religion, History, and Politics in Nigeria: Essays in Honor of Ogbu U. Kalu.* Chima J. Korie & G. Ugo Nwokeji (eds). New York: University Press of America, 2005.

27. Olunkunle, O. A. "The Impact of Religion on Nigeria Society: The Future Perspective." *Paper presented at the 25th annual Religious Conference.* Ibadan: University of Ibadan 17-20 September 1999.

28. Olupona, Jacob K. ed. *African Traditional Religion in Contemporary Society*. New
York: Paragon House, 1999.

29. Oranika, Paul. *Nigeria: One Nation, Two Systems*. Baltimore: Publish America,
2004.

30. Paden, John. *Faith and Politics in Nigeria*. Washington, D.C.: United States Institute of Peace Press, 2008

31. Panikkar, Raimundo. *The Intrareligious Dialogue*. New York: Paulist Press, 1999.

32. Pontifical Council for Inter-religious Dialogue. *Dialogue and Proclamation*. Rome:
Vatican Press, 1991.

33. Subair, Gbola. "Religious Crisis is Sheer Madness, says Sultan." *Nigerian Tribune*.
Abuja, November 12, 2009.

34. *The Basic Documents Vatican II: Constitutions, Decrees and Declarations*, Edited by 35. Austin Flanery, New York: Costello, Publishing Co., 1996

36. *The United Nations: Declaration on the Elimination of all form of Intolerance and of Discrimination based in Religion or Belief*, G.A. res. 36/55,36 U.N. GAOR Supp. (No. 51) at 171, U.N. Doc. A/36/684. 1981.

37. Trialogue – *Definition at your Dictionary*. http://www.yourdictionary.com/trialogue.

38. *United State Conference of Catholic Bishops' statement of the Jubilee Year 2000*.
http://www.usccb.org/ .

87